We Will Reap What We Sow

Reflections on Human Nature, Leadership and Feeding a Growing Population

Christophe Pelletier

ISBN: 1475101554
ISBN-13: 9781475101553

"The price of greatness is responsibility"
WINSTON CHURCHILL

CONTENTS

Preface

My first book, *Future Harvests*, focused on the challenges to meet the food demand of a growing world population. I had written it many months before it became a trendy topic in the media. I decided to write it because I could not find any similar book that took a comprehensive look at the many areas of food and farming. Most books and articles were either focused only on one particular area; or were biased and tried to promote one particular system. The book indicated which principles would be helpful to overcome the future challenges. It also presented many areas where food production and food supply have potential for improvement and optimization. In the conclusion of the book, I wrote the following sentences:

The answer to "Can we feed nine billion people by 2050?" is "Yes!" Will we feed nine billion people by 2050? That is a different question! It will all depend on everyone's attitude.

Future Harvests was mostly about facts and technical aspects. The future is not just about science and technology, though. The book sold well and copies are now on all continents. It brought me in contact with some of the readers. From our conversations, I felt a need to engage in a more philosophical reflection about the true role that human nature plays in securing food supply in the future.
"*We Will Reap What We Sow*" focuses on the human factor. Indeed, our attitude and the way we deal with problems will play an essential role in our future decisions.

The consequences of these decisions will shape our future world. Success or failure depends on us. The current level of technology, combined with the amazing developments that we can expect in the coming decades, is not the limiting factor. Our ability to act for the common good will determine our fate.

When I started my professional life, I strongly believed that the world had to revolve around technical and scientific knowledge. After all, my curriculum was all about mathematics, biology, physics and chemistry. After many years spent in sales, management and leadership positions, my views have changed profoundly. Although I remain very interested in all new scientific and technical progress, I also know that nothing happens unless people make it happen. I also know that interacting with people is everything but mechanical. Science and technology help developing superb tools and gaining amazing knowledge, but to become reality, people need to see the sense of these tools and to believe in them. Reaching people both in their minds and in their hearts is the only way to make a positive use of knowledge and science. Communication, honesty and respect are key ingredients for a successful future.

For those who have read *Future Harvests*, this book will be a useful sequel focusing on human nature, behavior, responsibility and leadership. The book will start where *Future Harvests* ended. This new book reviews the interaction between human population and their leaders, with all other aspects that contribute to food production and prosperity of societies. Those who have not read *Future Harvests* will find it a stimulating basis for discussions about the topic of feeding an increasing world population, and hopefully they will feel like read *Future Harvests*, too.

The true purpose of *We Will Reap What We Sow* is to make the reader think. It addresses the main questions that need to be answered. It discusses the pros and cons of different points of views. It indicates what the most likely consequences of different scenarios might be.

Human nature being as it is, the book also focuses on how to develop positive incentives and reduce the possibility of negative stimuli. *We Will Reap What We Sow* presents a balanced discussion between economic, scientific, technical, philosophical, and moral aspects. It describes how they contribute to build a prosperous future. In my opinion, it is important to integrate all these dimensions in the reflection. Food and agriculture are not only about technical performance. They are a reflection of society. They have a direct impact on health and environment and fill an ecological, social and emotional function too.

Not so long ago, people used to thank God before every meal for the food they had on the table. Nature was not always benevolent and food was precious. Nowadays, in developed countries, people do not feel this connection with Nature anymore. The fear of God forced some humility. This fear seems gone and in many areas, humans are playing God, at their own risk.

During the writing of *Future Harvests*, it became obvious to me how crucial the role of leadership is for future success. In the course of a number of assignments with my firm, this observation has grown even stronger. In order to be able to feed nine billion people, leadership is paramount. In this new book, I review the expectations that leaders will have to meet. The book discusses how leaders can help humankind overcome the fear of change and make the transition to a more food-secure world. Leaders will have to work towards eliminating practices that have no future. Dealing with change will be a major part of building the future world. Much has changed over the past decades. Much will change again in the future. The coming changes are beyond what most of us can imagine. Yet, it will happen. We had better accept it and prepare to adapt. It is not realistic to expect excesses to go on forever. In the coming evolution of our societies, we will have to give up certain things that we like. It is inevitable.

Unlike most of the articles published recently because of the media hype about the seventh billion human on Earth, *We Will Reap What We Sow* does not look for sensationalism. Doing that is quite easy. It may be entertaining, but it is not productive. Moreover, asking how we can feed seven billion people at a time when we have already passed this landmark is purely and simply futile. I will leave to others the fun of predicting the past and the present.

Just like *Future Harvests*, *We Will Reap What We Sow* will explore possibilities. It focuses on solutions, not on problems. There is no point of mongering fear. People do not get in orderly motion when they are afraid. Either they run in all directions or they freeze completely. Neither of these behaviors is useful to fix problems. Leaders are there to help people dare and succeed, not to hide afraid or give up hope. The task ahead is not easy, but it is not impossible. Only by realizing the benefits of responsible and collaborative action, will humanity ensure its future food security, and its future as a whole.

I wish you a happy reading!

Christophe Pelletier

INTRODUCTION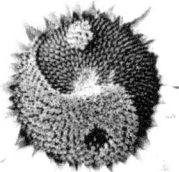

Believing in the Future

We Will Reap What We Sow

Believing in the Future

The recent economic crisis of 2008 and of the following years gives an example of how the perception of the future can change, and how the level of economic security affects human behavior. Before the economic crisis, many people in wealthy countries spent rather than saved. When the economic perspectives changed, so did their behavior. A similar behavior, but at business level, is the reluctance of companies to hire when the economic outlook is uncertain.

Readiness to act in order to build the future depends greatly on people's perception of what the word "future" means to them. The lucky ones who have comfortable lives actually do not think much about the future as a timeline. They consider the years to come as a given. They take the current situation for granted. When life is comfortable and feels safe, there is little incentive to change. Complacency has its risks. Inertia can be the cause of a future demise. On the opposite end of this, there are those who have no expectation of the future. For them, life is insecure for many reasons. It may be economic downturn, disease, violence or famine. All that matters is the here and now. Thinking ahead is almost impossible. The future is irrelevant. For those who live between these two extremes, the goal is to see life conditions improve. However, how this can be achieved, and whether it seems realistic depends greatly on the resources available.

Although many areas of the food and agricultural value chains need to be improved and can be improved, it is important to notice the resistance that many food security plans are facing during their execution. Obviously not all participants agree on the objectives and on the steps to follow.

This is especially important in developing countries where many problems affect food security, such as limited financial resources, limited water availability, post-harvest losses, difficult access to market or heavy bureaucracy to name a few. Individual short-term agendas tend to prevail and undermine action. To get people to believe in the future, the first step is to connect to their sense of what the future means to them, especially how long the future is.

For people who are 20 years old in a country where the life expectancy is 80, thinking about the future is quite normal. The life expectancy gives an indication of the period that the privileged ones have in mind. In regions where life prospects are dire, thinking even a couple of years ahead may be irrelevant. For some people, making it through the day is all that matters. However, even countries where insecurity and danger are present can believe in their future. When presenting a vision of the future, one must consider this way of thinking. The acceptance and the commitment to implement actions will depend largely on whether the timeline is perceived as reasonable. People are more inclined to participate when they think that they will be able to see the results in their lifetime.

Every year, a French poll institute, BVA-Gallup International, publishes a list of the countries where people are the most optimistic and where they are the most pessimistic. The 2012 survey came with surprising results. The most optimistic country was Nigeria, and the most pessimistic was France. Four African countries were in the Top 7 most optimistic. Overall, European countries were far from upbeat and many of them were at the bottom of the list.

On the way to the future, actions are always more convincing than words. Positive results need to appear soon. If they do not, the momentum in favor of the promised changes slows down. This is why a good strategy must start with the simpler and easier projects. They will deliver results faster. As success breeds success, they will generate more enthusiasm for the more difficult projects that require more time and more resources to be completed. This approach is a good way to build credibility and defuse criticism.

Another advantage is the increased level of awareness of the participants about what they can achieve, as they achieve more successes. This gain in confidence will boost the morale to pursue further improvements. This usually creates very healthy bottom-up dynamics that generates newer ideas on how to achieve the goals better and faster or even exceed them.

Clearly, increasing confidence requires actions at different levels. In the case of food security, the scope needs to go beyond agricultural development alone. Producing more food will not feed people if the hungry ones still do not make enough money to pay for food. Agriculture is only one of the economic sectors, and it will not produce miracles if it is not included in a more ambitious and broader goal.

Of all activities carried out to improve food security, the Chinese policies are rather interesting. The Chinese have a long-term-oriented culture. They are patient and persistent, as many episodes of their history demonstrate. Their development activities in Africa are comprehensive. Next to all their work to develop agricultural production, they also invest heavily in the development of small businesses. They are working to develop the local economy beyond just food production. Possibly, their experience of the last 30 years in developing the economy in China explains their approach. They know that social stability depends on people having at least the bare necessities. In the 1990s, the increasing demand for food products was the sign that China's goal was to feed its people first. In particular, the Chinese demand for wheat as well as for what Westerners considered not so appetizing animal by-products was strongly on the rise. The Chinese seem to have a similar approach with Africa. They understand that their food supply will be more secure if the countries where they invest are economically and socially stable. It is worth noting that China invests more money in Africa than all G8 countries together. It would appear that, to follow through with these policies, not having elections every few years allows them to execute a long-term vision without having to have interference of short-term interests.

On the other end of the spectrum, in terms of making people lose faith in the future, there is the example of Libyan land purchases in Mali. Local farmers, who had been working the land for themselves for all their lives, although the land did not belong to them, received notice that they had to leave their farms by the end of 2011. The owner had changed and there was no room for these farmers anymore. They have been evicted and there is no social plan or transition plan for them. They are losing their livelihoods. This kind of approach is exactly what could lead a country into civil war. By their accepting of such conditions, the landowners and the government show little long-term thinking. The future may teach them a hard lesson.

Businesses and non-profits that are active to develop food production need to nurture confidence in the execution of their plans. The owners, shareholders and fund providers must take a long-term approach to succeed. In such projects, the day-to-day share price on the stock exchange is not relevant. Such projects are long-term investments that will deliver a return only after many years. Among the most important investments, health and education play special and crucial roles. Without them, people cannot get any fulfilling occupation, and economic development lags.

Everyone who works in agriculture and food knows that there are about one billion people on Earth suffering from hunger. The temptation to think that the cause is a lack of food production is great, but it does not reflect the reality. Quite a few serious organizations and personalities claim that one Earth is not enough to feed nine billion people by 2050. Some claim that we would need two Earths. Others even go as far as mentioning the need for three, and even four, of our blue planet.

There are two possibilities with such statements. If they are true, then humanity has a problem, because there is only one Earth, and we will not get a second one. In such a case, the only way for supply and demand to get in balance is a reduction of the world's population, in a non-voluntary basis.

This could happen through famine, disease and/or wars. Since, in such a scenario, the maximum to the size of the world's population is lower than nine billion, once the limit number is reached, there must be a constant elimination of the people too many, through one of the means just mentioned. This is not a particularly happy thought. On the other hand, if such statements are erroneous, there is hope to feed the increasing world population with one Earth.

The path to feeding the world's population and to preserving agriculture's ability to provide adequate volumes is paved with many challenges. Leaders will have to show how to resolve the many issues that food production is facing or will face in the coming decades, and how to create a viable future.

As the population increases, the need for energy increases, too. Oil reserves are finite and new oilfields are becoming more and more difficult and expensive to exploit. It is only logical that oil will become more and more expensive in the future. To keep energy costs under control, the normal evolution is to develop equipment and vehicles that are more fuel-efficient. At the same time, oil that is more expensive also means that the relative price for alternative energy sources will become more competitive. In March 2011, an analyst from the bank HSBC published a report announcing that oil will no longer be available in 2060. In its future projections, the International Energy Agency (IEA) describes future energy sources as more diverse than they are now. They also mention that oil will not be the main source of energy anymore. Natural gas will take over. Some significant changes should be expected in the way agriculture uses energy, the type of machinery that farmers will use and how future logistics will be organized.

The change of economics in energy will affect fertilizers, too. The production of nitrogen fertilizers in particular uses large amounts of fossil fuel, essentially natural gas. On average, half of the nitrogen spread on fields is lost because of leaching. The focus will be on efficiency and on application strategies that are more efficient.

This is already happening with precision agriculture techniques. Next to this, the focus of the fertilizer industry should be on developing nitrogen fertilizers that are less sensitive to leaching. There would be an environmental advantage to do so.

In the area of environmental issues, climate change needs to be addressed more effectively than it has been so far. Regardless whether people believe in it, or believe it is caused by human activity or it is only a natural phenomenon, the number of severe climatic events is reason to consider countermeasures, just in case. The debate should not be about whether climate change is real or not. It is not about who may be responsible for it. True leaders take care of their people, and in this case, they should at least have scenarios, contingency plans and emergency preparedness plans. That is the least one can expect from those in positions of power and responsibility. In this case, the saying "the failure of the preparation is the preparation of failure" takes all its meaning.

Linked to climate to some extent, and a precious resource in all cases, water needs to be managed properly and carefully. For instance, all major river systems in Asia depend in part on Himalayan glaciers. If the glaciers were to disappear, the consequences could be catastrophic for the 2.5 billion people that depend on them. Further, as world agriculture uses 70% of all fresh water resources, growing food production will require more efficient water usage techniques. The focus must be on efficiency and on reduction of waste of water resources. Such objectives will require substantial financial resources and solid planning.

In the area of waste, food losses must be reduced as much and as diligently as possible. The moral issue of food being thrown away by the wealthy is obvious. The wealthy are not just in developed countries. In emerging countries, similar behavior is on the rise. The Indian government is considering fines for those who discard edible food.

In Western countries, where the percentage of food thrown away is the highest, governments are not considering introducing fines. The other food waste scandal is the post-harvest losses. The food is produced. It is edible, but because of a lack of proper infrastructure, it is left to rot. What a waste of seeds, land, water, money, labor and all other necessary inputs! The financial return to fix the problem is actually high and quick. There is plenty of work in this area for leaders. The first step to succeed in this is to recognize that no organization can fix this on its own. There is a need for collaborative leadership, because all the stakeholders in the food chains need to participate, and they all will reap the financial benefits of fixing post-harvest problems.

Food production is not a hobby. It is of the utmost importance for the stability and the prosperity of societies. Well-fed and happy people do not riot. The need to improve infrastructure and logistics is obvious. Food must be brought to those who need it. A proper transportation infrastructure is necessary. The choice of transportation methods has consequences for the cost of food supply and for the environmental cost as well. Road transport is relatively expensive and produces the highest amounts of greenhouse gases. Rail transport is already much better, and barge transport even better. The distance between production areas and consumption centers also needs to be looked at, together with the efficiency of logistics. The concentration of the population in urban centers, together with the change of economics in energy, will require a very different look on economic zoning, and on urban planning in particular. Optimization will be the name of the game. Completing the cycle of food and organic matter will become even more important than it is today, as the world's population is expected to concentrate further into urban centers. As humans are at the end of the food chain, many nutrients and organic matter accumulates where the human settlements are. The organic matter, as well as the nutrients, will have to be brought back to the land. This is essential to maintain soil fertility.

Phosphates mines are gradually running out. Phosphorus is an essential nutrient, and farmers will have to get it from somewhere. Today, many phosphates end up in waterways and eventually in the ocean. Other places where phosphates accumulate are sewage and manure, which are both going to play a pivotal role in soil fertility management, and farmland. Many farming areas show high levels of phosphates, and the nutrient status of the soil will have to be considered before adding more.

Special attention will be necessary to inform and educate consumers to eat better. Overconsumption, and the health problems that result from it, is already becoming a time bomb. Obesity is not only a Western problem. The same trend is appearing in many developing countries as well. Obesity is on the rise all over the world. The number of obesity cases in China, and even in some African countries, is increasing. The cost of fixing health is high, and it will be even more so in countries with an aging population, as age-related ailments add up to problems that are related to eating habits. Healthy societies are more productive and cost less to maintain.

As the economy grows, and wealth increases in more and more countries, diets are changing. Consumers shift from carbohydrate-based meals to a higher consumption of animal products, as well as fruit and vegetables. The "meat question" will not go away. Since it takes more than one kilogram of feed to produce one kilogram of animal product, increasing animal production adds even more pressure to produce adequate volumes of food. The question that will arise is how many animals the world can -or should- keep to produce animal products, and what species they should be.

Levels of production, and of demand, will result in price trends that will regulate production volumes to some extent, but government intervention to set production and consumption quotas cannot be excluded, either.

Similar questions will arise about biofuel production, especially the type of biofuel produced. There will be debates about the moral, economic, social and practical aspects of biofuels. The consequences on the price of food and animal feed cannot be ignored. The function of subsidies in the production of biofuels adds to this debate and there are strongly divergent points of view between the various stakeholders.

One of the most important issues in the discussion about feeding the world's population is food affordability. Producing more, and producing enough, is not enough. The food produced must be affordable, too. When this is not the case, people cannot buy enough food and they cannot eat. This is the main reason for malnourishment. To make food affordable, food production and the supply chain must be efficient. The costs of production need to be kept under control to avoid food inflation and/or farmers' bankruptcies.

In agriculture, just like in any other human activity, money always talks. Money is a powerful incentive, and when used properly, it is a powerful driver for improvement. Strategic use of financial incentives is part of policies. To meet the future challenges, leaders will have to develop the right kind of incentives. The focus will have to be on efficiency, on long-term continuity of production potential as well as on short-term performance. The financial incentives can be subsidies. Although the debates tend to make believe subsidies are all bad, there are good and useful subsidies. Another area of incentives to think about is the type of bonuses paid to executives. If the way executives are paid matters, the type of financial structure of businesses could influence the way they operate, too.

It should be no surprise when the question of whether food companies should be listed on the stock exchange arises. Short-term focus on the share price can be quite distracting from long-term objectives.

If elected officials are short term oriented because elections take place every four or five years, how do presentations of quarterly results to financial markets influence CEOs? The pressure by investors on companies' executive boards to deliver value is high. Investors on financial markets expect results within a relatively short period. After they take their profits, what happens to the companies' employees and what the long-term effects on the environment might be is irrelevant to them. This brings the question of the functioning of financial markets as a whole. What derivatives are acceptable? Who should be allowed to have access to which ones? What quantity should they be allowed to buy and sell? These questions and many more about financial markets will arise more and more loudly every time food prices will increase again in the future, and as social unrest may result from it.

To prepare for the future, it is important to prepare the generations of the future. Education will play a critical role in the success of societies. Countries will develop a strong middle class only by helping future generations to have access to knowledge, to develop skills and to train to fit in the jobs of the future. Through education, people can get better paying jobs. This allows them to buy adequate quantities of food for themselves and their families. Education is an investment to fight poverty and hunger. In the agricultural sector, it will be important to attract more young people to work in the food and agricultural sectors. In many countries, farmers are getting old and replacement is scarce.

These are just a few of the issues that the current and future leadership will have to solve to feed and preserve the world. Many discussions will take place about which systems are best suited to ensure prosperity and stability. The respective roles of governments, businesses, non-profits and of the people will certainly be reviewed with scrutiny.

PART I

Human Nature in a Changing World

Embrace Change!

Looking back is a good way to get a sense of how much may change in the future. It is easy to forget how life used to be. A quick look back at the past one hundred years shows the magnitude of the change.

One hundred years ago, the world was a different place. The world superpowers were in Europe. The Europeans had colonized Africa and large areas of Asia were under their control, too. There were still true declared Empires, meaning that they had Emperors and Empresses. Russia was one of them, as were Britain, Germany, Austria-Hungary, China, Japan and the Ottoman Empire. The United States were starting to play an important role, but they were far from being the dominant force. The world had not known any World War. Communism was only a doctrine, but it would soon change the world map and world politics for several decades, before almost disappearing completely. The world map looked different in 1912. Many borders have changed several times since then, and they will change again. There is no reason why borders that have been drawn arbitrarily by the superpowers at the end of World War I and II and after the wars of independence of the former European colonies would be carved in stone. The map of Africa, the Arab world, the Middle East, Central Asia and possibly the Indian sub-continent will look different in the future. Demographics, ethnic and religious issues, natural causes and economy will contribute to the change. These factors will translate in tensions about access to resources. Energy, water and food are already the most sensitive issues. They will only become more so as the world's population increases and develops economically.

Over the past one hundred years, the world of food production also changed dramatically. Here are some of the past milestones that have shaped food production, food supply and consumption, as we know it today.

One century ago, the world's population was about 1.750 billion people. By then, the prospect of nine billion people on Earth was not even thinkable. Environmental concerns did not exist. Food security was present nowhere at all. Times were completely different. The Industrial Revolution had started a few decades earlier, powered by coal. People were frugal because they had no other choice. The era of mass production and mass wastage had not come, yet. Cars were only for the wealthy. Commercial airlines did not even exist. The Dutch company KLM would be the first to be created in 1920. Louis Blériot had just performed the airborne crossing of the English Channel in 1909, and the crossing of the Atlantic Ocean by Charles Lindbergh Jr would happen only in 1927. The chemical industry was at its early stages, but soon World War I would offer a horrible opportunity to test the lethal effects of some of its products. Fortunately, there are many positive applications of chemistry, too.

Industrial production of nitrogen fertilizers had just been developed. In 1905, the Norwegian company Yara was the first to produce and commercialize calcium nitrate. By then, the positive effect on yields surprised many observers and immediately, mineral fertilizers became very popular with farmers. One century later, because of the overuse of nitrates, the former wonder meets more criticism. This does not take away that mineral fertilizers have contributed significantly to higher yields. The discussion of how to use them more effectively and reduce their environmental impact is critical for the future of food production just as well.

Another little revolution took place in 1922, when the Swedish company Electrolux commercialized home refrigerators on a large scale. This invention, as well as all other refrigeration equipment, has helped preserve food longer and better. It has also contributed to the change of the whole food supply chain. Refrigeration has also contributed to some negative side effects.

It has contributed to longer distances between farm and table, thus supporting road transport and its negative effect on the environment. There probably would be no perishables in supermarkets if refrigeration did not exist. Distribution channels would be different.

In 1928, a happy accident happened. While Alexander Fleming was studying the properties of staphylococci, he was not looking to find out anything about antibiotics. The accidental presence of a fungus among some of his bacteria culture changed the nature of his work and of medicine. Before penicillin, an infection could be fatal. This is a good reason to make sure that antibiotics will keep working. The development of antibiotic-resistant bacteria is a very serious threat. Animal husbandry is a major user of antibiotics. Without antibiotics, there would never have been intensive animal production, and there would never have been such a level of consumption of animal products as there is today. The regular food recalls because of bacterial contamination are a reminder that bacteria are present in our food chain. Food safety is a serious matter. This is part of feeding the world, too.

That same year, an experiment carried out by Frederick Griffith showed that DNA carries genetic information. Although it would take another 25 years before Watson and Crick discovered the double helix structure of DNA, the stage was set for further discoveries and applications. In this area, too, the use of science and technology can lead to controversies. Knowledge about genetics is interesting because it also shows the value of experience. Even if science could not describe why traits were hereditary, farmers had improved plants and animals for a long time by selecting the best individuals for the characteristics that mattered to the farmers. The concept of science-based is good, but it is sometimes possible to achieve progress without knowing all the details. This also implies that waiting until all the scientific knowledge is gathered can actually delay progress.

A couple of years later, in 1930, the first supermarket opened. Supermarkets have dramatically changed the way food and all other consumer goods are sold. The combination of cheap oil, the development of automobiles, the ability to have a one-stop shop experience have shaped more than just consumption. They have contributed to urban planning and life at home. Today, most shoppers who buy food at the supermarket have lost the connection between where and how food is produced, as well as their perception of what food is.

At about the same time, a restaurant, White Castle, initiated and developed the principles of fast food. Ten years later, in 1940, the first MacDonald's restaurant opened in San Bernardino, California. Originally not a fast food restaurant, it gained popularity when it moved to speed service in 1948. The rest is history. Fast food restaurants are present almost everywhere. Originally, consumption of fast food did not cause any particular problem. The image and the perception were good. In these times, overconsumption of food was more the exception than the rule. Fast food was fine. Portions were reasonable.

In 1939, another element of modern agriculture appeared. DDT was the first chemical pesticide. It worked quite well, but serious side effects appeared. Although DDT is still used in some countries, usually to fight malaria or yellow fever, other chemicals have replaced it in agriculture. Herbicides appeared later, in the late 1940s. All chemicals of both groups still are a source of controversy. Managing both the short-term effects, which are mostly their effectiveness to kill pests and weeds, and the long-term effects on potential risks on human health and environment is not an easy task. It all comes down to the assessment of the risks, risks for food production and risks for the society.

Electronics is another area where a real revolution has taken place. A century ago, very few people had access to a phone. Communications were slower than they are today.

The ability to process information was also much slower. There were no computers, as they appeared in the 1940s, and they were not portable. Calculations had to be done manually. Pencil and paper were among the main tools. With the development of computers and telecommunications, the same tasks can be completed much more quickly. The fast access to information resulting from this progress allows everybody from the farm to the consumer to make faster and, when done well, better decisions. So far, the internet that became available to the public in 1995 has played the dominant role as a platform that supports all other developments in the area of information access. Theoretically, the ability to make better decisions should result in doing the right thing more frequently. However, the human factor with all its desires and fears does not always follow the same rational and mechanical process.

Over the past one hundred years, much has changed, and so have demographics. The world's population is increasing fast, and the challenge remains the same: how can humanity sustain itself? The fear of running out of resources, and especially food has been here for a long time. Malthus would have never believed that seven billion people could live on Earth. This is the good news. Humans can achieve more than they think.

When thinking of the challenges that lie ahead, trying to envision some of the things to come is a good exercise. Of course, nobody can predict the future, but a number of facts and trends can help determine some scenarios. An interesting way of imagining how much change will come is to look at new products. According to estimates, about 60% of the products that exist today did not exist 10 years ago.

By extrapolating this factor for the coming decades and assuming that in 10 years from now 60% of the products that will be available do not exist today, the result is simply amazing.

About 97% of the products that would exist in 2050 do not exist today, and by 2100, this number would be as high as 99.9%! Actually, this calculation is not completely accurate, because nothing predicts that the change factor of 60% would be random. Some products are more important than others are. Gadgets will have a higher turnover ratio than essential products. Nonetheless, it sounds reasonable to state that between 60% and 99.9% of the products in 2100 do not exist today. What will be the products of the future? This is impossible to say. Otherwise, they probably would already exist. Exact numbers are not that important. What is important is that it is not possible to think about the coming decades by looking at the present. What exists today will be just a minor part of tomorrow. Resisting change is a futile exercise. When it comes to food production, there is no reason to think that the current production systems will be relevant in the future. To succeed and meet the challenges of an increasing population, it is necessary to keep an open mind. The economics of agriculture will change, because the economics of all the resources and the dynamics of the markets will change. Clinging to the present or to the past is useless, but learning from the present and the past is one of the most important things to do. Only by understanding the consequences of past decisions and actions, will humanity be able to improve and succeed.

The size of the world's population is among the most significant changes for the future. There are many challenges, as the media tell us on a daily basis, but there are many opportunities, too. The first and the main of these opportunities is the population growth. In the coming four decades, there will be two billion more people to feed. Never before has humanity seen such a demand increase. Farmers and food suppliers do not have to worry about a lack of market opportunities. Not only the number of people will increase, but the consumption pattern will change, too. Until recently, most of the consumption took place in developed countries, mostly the USA, the EU and Japan.

For the coming decades, food consumption in these areas will not increase. There are simple reasons for this. One is the demographic stagnation of industrialized regions.

Another reason is that people of these regions already eat too much. They have no room for more consumption. At best, they can replace one food by another. In emerging countries, economic growth results in the rise of a new middle class. A change of diet is the first change that takes place when the standard of living increases. People switch from staple foods such as rice or bread to higher quantities of animal protein and more fruit and vegetables.

The OECD (Organization for Economic Cooperation and Development) looked at the future evolution of the respective shares of consumption by the middle class, between different regions of the world over the period 2000-2050. Their study was for consumption goods at large. The graph is quite impressive.

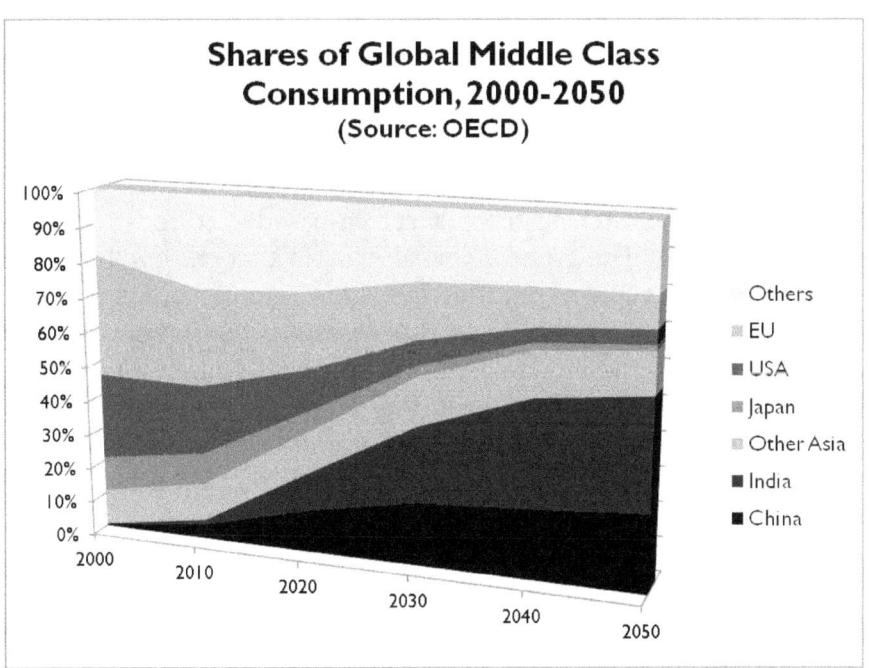

The relative share of Western countries will shrink dramatically. While in 2000 the USA represented about 5% of the world's population and consumed about 25% of the world resources, they will represent only about 4% of the population and consume about 4% as well by 2050.

A similar evolution will take place in the EU and in Japan. China and India show the opposite trend. With a share of the total world consumption close to negligible percentages a few years ago, their economic development and the size of their middle classes will transform consumption markets dramatically. Estimates are that the middle class from China and India combined will represent about 45% of the world middle class by 2030!

Market demand, and therefore world prices, will be dictated by the demand from these two countries and not by Western countries anymore. The graph covers all consumption items. The situation for food alone might show some differences, but the trend would show a similar pattern. The demand for food in emerging countries will grow strongly. In 2011, China became the world's largest grocery market, passing the USA. By 2015, Brazil, India and Russia should also join the top 5 grocery markets, and Indonesia should enter the top 10. The increase in consumption will not affect only volumes but also the type of food. The change in the type of food that consumers of the middle class of emerging countries will demand will go beyond switching from a starch-based diet to an animal-protein-rich diet. The type of animal protein that they will eat will change, too. A couple of decades ago, China would import many of the low quality animal products that Western consumers did not want to eat. The new middle class is much less hungry for those low-quality products. They want the prime cuts, too. Instead of being complementary, emerging markets and developed countries will be in competition with each other for the better animal products. This will have profound consequences for the future. It will make the sale of the low-quality products more difficult. At the same time, it will make the demand for prime products explode, pushing prices up even more.

Western consumers and Western markets used to set the prices. In the future, Western consumers will have to buy food based on the price set in Asia. This change will make producers and buyers look at business opportunities in a completely different manner than they currently do.

All emerging countries show the same trend. Brazil now sees domestic demand for chicken meat increase faster than export markets. The same happens for seafood. While their traditional market for Atlantic salmon was the US market, Chilean salmon farmers see growing possibilities in the Brazilian market. Since air transport from Chile to the USA is quite expensive, and more expensive than transport to Brazil, the trade flow will change. Norwegian salmon might become a better alternative for US buyers, but the Chinese are now buying increasing quantities. American buyers must prepare themselves to pay much more than in the past for salmon products.

It becomes clear that the challenge of feeding the world depends for a large part on future consumption of animal protein. The increase of human consumption of grains will be relatively limited. Considering that in 2011, animal feed uses more than a third of all grains produced, more production of animal protein will put much more pressure on the markets of agricultural commodities.

Producing enough to meet the desires of a more affluent world population is actually about allowing the luxury of eating more meat than people really need. If emerging markets are increasing their demand for animal protein, the situation will be different in developed countries. Because consumers in the latter countries eat already more than enough, and because the populations of these countries are aging, consumption will not increase. The focus will shift further to quality before quantity. Actually, food consumption per capita will probably decrease, and consumption of meat per capita will decrease the most. A part of meat consumption will happen in festive and rarer occasions. The price will not matter, or if it does, portions will simply be smaller. After all, a drop of an ounce (28 g) per portion would not make much of a difference for sensory satisfaction. High-end restaurants serve smaller portions. The focus for this type of consumption will be about production systems. Consumers will look increasingly for naturally raised and fed animal products, as well as about the welfare of farm animals. In the USA, this would have been almost unthinkable even a decade ago, but it is already moving in this direction.

In Europe, the trend started earlier. Animal welfare is becoming an issue in more and more countries, such as in China. One of the hot topics that started 10 to 15 years ago is GMO (genetically modified organisms). The European buyers wanted strict guarantees that there would be no GMOs in animal feed. They would audit their suppliers on a regular basis about all sorts of production techniques and procedures at least once a year. In the USA, the reaction was more one of "GM what?" American consumers were not paying attention to that issue and apparently did not care about it. Things have changed. The food movement is growing in all urban centers. Consumers question industrial agriculture production systems. GMOs have become an activist topic. The dynamics for change are here, and they will not go away. A new trend has emerged over the past decade. In 25 years from now, the American market will be different from what it is today, and so will European, Asian and African markets.

The way people buy their food and other goods is very likely to change, too. The model of malls, supermarkets and fast food restaurants developed because of cheap energy, and in particular cheap gasoline. The economy is built on the ability to move goods over long distances quickly because of cheap oil. The modern way of life, just like the nature of the goods consumers buy, depends on cheap and quick transportation, and on cheap labor. There is no reason to think that this model will keep making economic sense forever. Energy will become more expensive. Actually, it will become much more expensive than it is today. The energy markets have already gone up, but this is only the beginning.

The world's population is not just growing, but it is also becoming wealthier. More and more people are able to afford the lifestyle of industrialized countries. China should grow its middle class to about 650 million people by 2030. India's middle class should reach close to 600 million people by then. The number of people with more disposable income will increase in all developing countries.

If the Western lifestyle is the norm, it is clear that demand for all commodities will rise very significantly. It does not matter whether there would be enough raw materials to produce all the goods that the future world's middle class can buy. For non-renewable commodities, such as fossil fuels, the increase of demand for finite resources will have only one outcome: a strong price increase. Moreover, all the money printing caused by the financial crisis will eventually lead to inflation, especially for the countries where the currencies will have eroded over time. The effect of inflation will be hard felt. This is not all. Emerging countries have developed for a large part because of the relocation of manufacturing and services. The low wages that their workforce was ready to accept has contributed to the production of cheap goods. As the economy is growing and as the next generations are better educated than their parents were, people can find better paying jobs. Wages will increase there, too.

This takes away the competitive advantage for the production units located in these countries. Then, it is easy to realize that raw materials that will become more expensive because of supply and demand, combined with a more expensive workforce, will lead to goods that are more expensive to produce. Of course, there is always the possibility of relocating manufacturing units again. The region where the workforce will be the cheapest might be Africa. As the 21st century sees the rise of Asia, the 22nd century could be the century of Africa. It could follow a similar patter to what has happened in Asia. Countries that have depended a lot on manufacturing to grow their economies, such as China, will face new competition. The West faces the prospect of losing more of its economic strength. The aging population that wants wages that are not competitive, but faces expensive benefits and social security costs will have to rethink its model. Wages will decrease in the current developed countries, and disposable income will not be as high as it used to be.

Yes, there will be change. Although feeding nine billion people is the topic that receives the most attention, another question needs to be answered.

With two billion more people, many new jobs will have to be created. What will these jobs be? Before, the Great Recession of 2008, 70% of the GDP in the USA was retail. In the coming five to ten decades, will this still be the dominant model? With the end of cheap oil, the old model of roads, parking lots, malls and drive-through will probably change. One can wonder if there still will be malls and large grocery stores. With the growth of online sales, it is quite possible than instead of having shoppers going to the goods, the dominant model will be one of goods coming to the consumers. With the end of cheap oil, urban planning will change, too. It is likely that logistics will undergo a profound change. Logistics will be adapted to a new situation. The location of where people live and work will change. The way they live and work will change. It seems reasonable to think that the supply chain from producer to consumer will change for all goods. Home delivery could become the more competitive alternative to traffic jams and crowded stores. There is no reason why urban transportation would not undergo some significant changes, too. It is conceivable that online activity will grow further.

If the proper systems are developed, it should be possible to work from home while enjoying similar interaction to an actual shared workplace. The same could happen for education. It should be possible to recreate virtual classrooms where students can have a similar experience as in actual school buildings, but from home. The savings in terms of time and fuel would be substantial.

The German automaker BMW, the products of which have embodied success and individualism, is now working on a vehicle-sharing concept. Car co-ops are growing in many cities.

An area that gets the futurist community excited is the development of 3-D printers. These printers are somehow similar to printers that print out text from the home computer, but as their name indicates, they are able to print in height, too. They have been in use for some time already in manufacturing for the development of prototypes. They help build models for industrial testing at a much lower cost than the former traditional prototypes.

A new generation of 3-D printers is arriving on the market for prices as low as US$5,000. They used to cost more than US$100,000 only a few years ago. What do these machines do? They build objects by printing them layer by layer. They work with computer software that has all the product specifications and all the parameters of the object to build. The users only need to download the product software in their computers and click on "Print" to start production. Three-dimensional printers are still in their early stages, but they already can produce objects, such as tools or spare parts.

The company EADS, which owns Airbus Aerospace, produced a bicycle in one printing jet. The bicycle works exactly like a traditional one. The component used to print it is light and extremely solid. The next step could be airplane parts or maybe even an entire plane.

Such printers are already used in a number of professional areas. For instance, it is possible to build prosthetics that are tailor-made for the patient.

These printers promise so much that researchers are currently trying to develop the possibility of using biological material as the printing "ink" to build organs. The idea is that individuals could grow their own biological tissues from their own cells, and "print out" replacement organs in case of accidents or of health problems. A group from Cornell University in New York is currently working on this. In late 2011, a group from Germany's Fraunhofer Research Institute was successful at printing biocompatible blood vessels. Researchers from Washington State University have been able to print bone-like material that can stimulate bone growth once implanted. These printers are not for industrial or professional purposes only. The home version can already make all sorts of objects, from whistles to pliers via almost any gadget that shoppers can buy at the supermarket. All that the user would need is to have the compound that is needed to produce the object at home. These printers have the potential to revolutionize production and consumption of goods.

There would be no need to have plants standardizing the mass production of goods. People could build them when they need them. There is no need for wholesalers or retailers in this model. There is no need to ship goods over long distances, either. Some people envision the possibility to print food this way. Is this how profound future change will be? It is very possible.

Future technological possibilities are amazing, and farming will undergo major changes in the future, too. The average age of farmers is increasing everywhere around the world, creating the question of who will take over and what effect it will have on the future of agriculture and future production systems. One of the possibilities to compensate the loss of farmers and workforce in agriculture is the development of robots. Because of the lack of interest of youth to take over farms, the Japanese are actively working on setting up farms that could be run by robots, instead of humans.

In many other countries, the aging farming population and the limited interest from younger people to become farmers, also linked to the rising price of agricultural land, raises the question of how big farms might become, and how to manage them. Currently, many developments in the field of robotics, of satellite applications, of field sensors and of computer programs make a futuristic picture of farming become more realistic.

Although it is still a rather new concept, precision agriculture is the future. With the expected rise of the cost of energy and of the price of all compounds made with massive use of fossil fuels, the name of the game will be to produce with zero waste. Future economics will not allow for wasting energy, water or fertilizers or any other input. It will be imperative to get the most out of the least, not just simply producing more with less.

The use of satellites to map fields and indicate the variation of the content of fertilizing elements in the soil is already a reality. The use of GPS for harvesting is now common with modern equipment.

Farmers are only one step away from having computers processing all this data and operating fertilizer spreaders by automatically regulating the distribution of fertilizer on the field, based on the soil scan assessment. This will avoid overuse of fertilizer in zones that already contain enough nutrients. With the depletion of phosphate mines, and the large variation of phosphate contents in soil, it will pay off.

Technological advances are also only one step away from designing tractors, harvesters and other agricultural equipment to do the work in the fields without drivers. Kinze, a company from Iowa, is already developing such a technology. Harvesting can be carried out without a tractor operator, as the GPS system can position the tractor with the bin next to the combine harvester. They also have developed a tractor operator-free planter. Such systems will change the tasks of human operators. They will allow farmers to manage much larger areas from one remote location. Their role would become more one of process controller, monitoring and steering the machines by ways of cameras and remote control.

Maybe a farmer will be able to monitor several fields at the same time from his/her office, miles away from the fields. This also would require less physical work, thus allowing aging farmers to manage at least as much production as they would have at a younger age. This would become even more of a possibility, as farming robots would be developed to replace humans for the physically more demanding activities. If it happens, it is still difficult to know what such robots would look like. Perhaps, the Prospero model gives a first indication. Insects, birds and fish inspired the design of the Prospero robot. The robot walks and looks like a crab. According to the builder and developer, David Dourhout, the robots work in teams, communicate with each other and can perform most of the activities of a farmer. They can plant, fertilize and spray crop protection products through small tubes to apply the exact amount of product that the plants need. There is no waste of inputs.

Sensors also would help farmers detect potential threats at an earlier stage, even before they actually become visible to the human eye. This would allow starting treatment before problems could take proportions that would threaten production. This has the potential to help farmers produce more optimally, and to produce higher yields than they would otherwise. Developments in the area of sensors also offer many possibilities in terms of farm and risk management. The ability to monitor variations of temperature, humidity, plant growth, the presence of diseases, fungi and other pests in real time would help use resources much more efficiently. In 2009, the Oklahoma State University developed the Green Seeker. The machine roams the fields. It scans the plants with an infrared and near-infrared beam. Depending on how the plants reflect the light back to the sensors, the machine can assess their physiological needs. Then, it can distribute the exact amount of fertilizer or herbicide needed. It reduces the amount of products spread on the field and in the environment while maximizing their efficiency, just as the Prospero intends to do.

Linking such sensors to devices that can release the necessary amounts of water, nutrients and pesticides would help produce quite efficiently, and would reduce the use of inputs. This would help reduce waste, work towards more sustainable farming methods and reduce the use of chemicals. If those still exist as a production aid, they would be used only at the right time, at the right place and in the right quantities, instead of being applied systematically to the whole fields, including areas where they are not needed. The use of airplanes to spread chemicals will probably be eliminated in the future, which would also reduce the use of fossil fuels. Instead of airplanes that consume substantial amounts of fossil fuels, it is possible to think that energy-efficient solar-powered drones would have a "patrolling" function to detect anomalies or the extension of pests in the fields.

The spy hummingbird drone[1] is already functioning. It has the shape and the size of a hummingbird and the operator can have a view from the bird's head via a micro camera. Perhaps, the farm drones will look like bees. After all, the robot bee is also in development. The robotic earthworm is also in the works. The purpose of these "robo-worms" would be to help decontaminate the soils of chemicals and metals. By using the huge amount of data that these robots, sensors and drones would produce, fields and their ecosystems would be monitored on a continuous basis. Decision-making would be faster than today. Corrective action could be implemented automatically as well.

By adding more monitoring functions and developing ecological modeling, this futuristic approach would be a way of managing the interaction between the crops and the ecosystem. That is one of the purposes of food production. Managing the ecosystem surrounding the fields would ensure that production is carried out in an environmentally sustainable manner. Monitoring living organisms in and outside the fields would help optimizing production. The farmer would know the status of soil organisms, mostly worms, insects and microorganisms. He would be able to deal with pests in a targeted manner, almost in a similar way as the images of surgical strikes that we can see in the news. Mapping the extent of weeds through such devices would also allow their control in a targeted manner and with minimal use of potentially harmful compounds. The emphasis would be about control and management, not on killing out everything that seems a threat.

Monitoring fields in this way would support the role of farmers as environmental stewards, while making this task easier to execute as well. Farmers would have timely information about production effects on groundwater quality and possible residues in the soil and the crops. They could take action, and they could have the data to record what they do.

---

[1] The US company AeroVironment from Monrovia, California has developed it. It supplies the US military with unmanned drones.

Of course, this may sound like a bit of science fiction, but considering the amazing innovations taking place in the all the areas mentioned, together with the constant miniaturization of devices and the increased processing abilities of computers, it might not be as far-fetched as it may seem. Farming in the coming decades will look different than it does today. Thinking about the scope of possibilities and their effect on tomorrow's world is very helpful to prepare to the future. It is necessary to do it as early as possible, because it takes time to be ready to determine how society will look in the coming decades. Now is the time to think about what the future roles of humans will be, what jobs they will have and on which model the economy will run.

When Human Nature Gets in the Way

Feeding the world goes much further than just a technical challenge. Of course, production can be more efficient, infrastructure can be developed and new technologies may be able to help improve the situation. In most discussions, one particular aspect seems to be neglected, unless it is taken for granted: the human factor. Getting things done is not just about having the tools. To succeed, those who have to make it happen need to have the skills and they need to know what is expected from them. The economy exists only because humans exist. It is shaped by and it evolves because of the actions of people. Human activities and decisions have roots in many dimensions. Values and beliefs in ethical, moral, economic, social, religious, cultural, environmental and political areas influence their judgment and their actions. Everything has consequences. So does inaction.

The road to ensure food security for all is still long. Although humans are very creative in solving and overcoming their problems, when it comes to food production, they still lack control of many parameters. Since the beginning of agriculture, farmers have looked to the sky to see what the weather would bring them. Rituals to call for friendly climatic conditions and soil fertility were common in all cultures. Droughts, floods, never-ending rainfall, frost and other climatic events have happened on an ongoing basis and, climate change or not, they still will happen in the future. Before looking at how to overcome the challenges to meet future food demand, identifying the reasons that can hinder success is a useful exercise. People have demonstrated in the past their ability to overcome many crises, but human nature has its flaws. Some of them can be impediments to succeed in the task ahead.

Without trying to take a religious approach, it is interesting to notice that most of the reasons why the world might fail at feeding itself lie in the so-called seven deadly sins. Actually, the deadly sins reflect some of the most fundamental needs of human beings. They become sins when the needs become compulsive and uncontrollable urges. In no particular order, the seven deadly sins are gluttony, greed, pride, sloth, envy, wrath and lust. They are respectively related to the needs for food security, financial security, self-respect, comfort, belonging to a group, justice, and last but not least, sex. Except for wrath, the deadly sins are about selfishness and self-interest. Selfishness is the ultimate form of poverty of the soul. It is a sign that one has nothing to offer to the world. The world's ability to feed itself depends on factors influencing supply and demand. There are many challenges on the supply side, mostly because of the level of demand, and in particular of the nature of the demand.

In 2011, The Global Burden of Metabolic Risk Factors of Chronic Diseases Collaborating Group published a study showing that the population of more and more countries is getting fatter and increasingly exposed to diet-related illnesses. It is the sign that they eat more than they should. The extreme cases of compulsive snacking and the increased consumption of animal protein that requires more feed to feed the animals than the same amount would feed humans add to the problem. Rich diets as a daily state of affairs challenge the ability of farmers of basic agricultural commodities to keep up with demand. As the number of people showing signs of gluttony increases, the imbalance between supply and demand becomes greater than with a healthy and balanced diet.

A little bit of greed is good, as it stimulates action and entrepreneurship. It is a strong driver for people to take risks for the sake of material reward. It encourages the action that the challenges ahead require. It also helps money flowing into the economy. Projects are developed and new activity increases. To succeed in the future, the world will need plenty of such a drive.

The problem with greed is that the focus shifts to the short-term financial reward. Greed is also essential to ensure the continuity of food production for the long term, and people should not engage in solutions that can undermine future food security. Speculation, one of the purest forms of greed, will have to be brought under control. Its consequences in terms of social unrest and on the stability of societies are too serious.

Ironically, a little bit of fear will help create some balance. Fear is greed's twin sibling. Although fear is a defense mechanism, it will not protect humanity from food shortages. There are many fears that play a role in people's perception of food production. The fear of new technological developments and their long-term effect is a cause of strong resistance to move forward. Yet, a number of areas in agriculture and food production need to undergo changes. In markets, fear can also cause major crises. If the fear of a food shortage spreads, prices of agricultural commodities can skyrocket. Speculators thrive on other people's fears. The problem is not so much fear itself as it is the inability to overcome fear and to start finding effective solutions to the problems. When dealing with novelty and change, it is essential to carry out thorough and objective research before taking a position. Concerns need to come with alternative solutions. Only through communication and dialogue is it possible to bring the debate to a more rational level where all participants can contribute their knowledge and experience to a constructive progress. Erratic behavior and inaction will not be helpful. To feed nine billion people, the world can neither be passive nor yield to panic.

Another human trait that can cause damage is ego, a major component of pride. Unfortunately, ego is rather common. Because some people seem to have difficulties to admit being wrong, to admit that they sometimes do not have all the answers, they have a tendency to wage turf wars, which undermines win-win possibilities. Turf wars may end up with a winner, but usually it is a Pyrrhic victory. Often, the lose-lose situation that arises will stand in the way of future projects.

There is nothing wrong for anyone to know that he/she does not know something. Nobody knows everything. Acknowledging one's ignorance is the first step to learning, therefore improving. Always being right is very rare, and believing otherwise is usually rather delusional. It shows a lack of sense of reality. There is nothing like some good old-fashioned ego to thwart the general interest. Thinking that one can win only if the others lose shows little empathy. When it comes to food security for nine billion people, a short-term victory at someone else's expense will soon be a defeat for all. Interest groups tend to act like this, though. Such a mindset can be potentially dangerous. For as much as it is essential that all opinions and philosophies be expressed, it is just as essential to have and show empathy and respect for those who think differently.

A healthy democracy needs strong different opinions, and it works well as long as the different parties truly want a democratic process. Without genuine dialogue and debate, there is no democracy. Interest groups tend to act like self-interest groups, especially in cultures that are polarized. Cultures that nurture consensus have less of a problem. The objective of interest groups is to influence policies. In countries where politicians depend on these groups for the funding of their campaigns, the relationship between politicians and interest groups seems reminiscent of corruption and of banana republics. It is no surprise that citizens have lost trust in politics and in corporations. There is conflict of interest, and it is not in the interest of the public.

Bribery is not appreciated everywhere, though. For instance, the case during 2011 of the three members of the European Parliament who were willing to take bribes from journalists of the Sunday Times, disguised as lobbyists, in exchange for watered down legislation on bank reform legislation shows that. After being exposed, and despite their poor and predictable bad faith arguments, the three had no choice than to resign.

Complacency, another symptom of pride mixed with sloth, is a danger as well. The number of countries that claim, through their professional associations and governments, to have the highest standards in the world is amazing. They all claim the number one position in fields as diverse as food safety, environment, sustainability, productivity or efficiency. Those who have travelled know that no country is completely above the rest. Many countries have good procedures and regulations in place, but they all can improve in the areas they claim to lead. It does not take much to go backwards.

Modern societies have grown increasingly individualistic and materialistic. The focus has shifted towards the short term, with instant gratification being the most extreme example. Attention spans have shrunk dramatically. Indifference and lack of compassion are common. When it comes to ensuring food security for nine billion people, this attitude will work adversely.

There are many possibilities to produce enough food, but there is still a lot of work to do to achieve the goal. Sloth manifests with a number of bad habits. Throwing large amounts of food in the garbage is one of those bad habits. By changing behaviors, it is possible to save amazing quantities of food. First, the *I-do-not-care* attitude must become the exception, not the rule. Large quantities of food are lost before reaching markets in developing countries. All it takes to solve the problem is to make the funds available. Compared with the stimulus packages and bank bailouts, the amount is ridiculously low. There too, the *not-my-problem* attitude is unacceptable. Humans are social animals. This behavior has been an evolutionary advantage that has ensured the survival of the species. Hard-nosed individualism and indifference go in the opposite direction. They work only in periods of abundance. By showing some compassion and helping others succeed, the fortunate ones actually increase their own odds of survival. In a globally interconnected world, any negative food security event affects the entire world, eventually. If things seem dire while there are "only" seven billion people on Earth, there can be no doubt of how painful it might be with nine billion.

Together with the slow disappearance of common sense, not addressing the right issues is another growing tendency that can hinder the attempts to feed nine billion people in a few decades. Too often, the focus is on eliminating the symptom rather than the cause of the problem. This usually results in creating a new set of unnecessary problems. By eliminating the cause of a problem, the solution is less likely to create a new problem.

An example that illustrates this is the pill to burn fat. The pill focuses on the symptom only and gives the hope that it will fix the problem. The source of the problem remains and then the pill appears to have negative side effects, creating new problems to solve with another pill. The actual problem is that the person eats too much and gets fat. The solution should be to eat less and better.

In the case of food security, an example of mistaking the cause and the symptom is hunger. The cause is poverty, much more than the lack of food. The food may not be there exactly, but it is there somewhere. Unfortunately, the poor cannot afford it. Therefore, the food will not come to them. Considering the complexity of food production, finding the true causes of problems is not easy. It could be compared with the layers of an onion. The symptoms are the outer layers. Solutions that address symptoms only add layers, increasing the complexity even further. It is important to be able to see towards the core of the onion. Although analysis may be boring sometimes, it is an absolute necessity to solve problems effectively.

There are many plans for food security out there. Almost every government has one. Industry groups come out with their vision as well. So do environmental groups. There is no lack of objectives. There may be too many of them, actually. Often, the problem is the failure of the execution. To achieve food security, proper execution is paramount. It requires much more than a vision and a plan on paper. It requires a clear allocation of responsibilities and a schedule for the delivery of the objectives. It requires good and strong leadership.

Often, what undermines the execution of a plan is the lack of a sense of ownership of the mission. All the actors involved in food security need to be involved as early as possible in the process. They must participate in the set-up of the plan. It increases their level of commitment.

Every time that an important player in the plan is not fully committed, the project is undermined. All the people involved must realize why it is important, and especially why it is important to them. There is nothing worse than a plan developed by a limited group that tries to push it onto those who actually must make it happen. When people do not feel that they have some ownership of the plan, they simply do not participate fully. Next to a sense of ownership, skills are essential. Since they will have to produce as much food as possible efficiently and sustainably, farmers and potential farmers need to have access to proper education and training. In order to improve and produce both more and better, they need to have the knowledge and the possibility to update this knowledge. This may seem obvious in rich countries where education and training are well organized, but in many developing nations, usually plagued with food insecurity, this is not the case. Too often, even the most basic knowledge is missing. For these populations to succeed and to increase food security, it is necessary to have education high on the list of priorities.

Farmers must have access to knowledge and they must be able to become always better at what they do. It is in the interest of every person in the world, regardless of where he/she lives. Having skilled farmers is one thing, but it is as important to have farmers for the future, too. To have food, the world needs farmers. To have farmers, it is necessary to make the profession attractive and economically viable. In many countries, the average age of farmers is high and there seems to be little interest from the youth to take over. In the USA, the average of farmers was 58 in 2011. It is 66 in Japan. In South Africa, the typical farmer is between 58 and 62 years old. In the EU, there are more than 4.5 million farmers older than 65, while there are fewer than one million farmers younger than 35. This latter group represents only 6% of EU's farmers. This is how serious the situation is becoming.

To overcome the challenges, having good, motivated, and trained workers is not enough. Someone needs to show the way forward and make the right things happen. Leadership is paramount in any human endeavor. It will be even more so for the goal of feeding nine billion people. Technology is not the limiting factor. All success stories have one thing in common. They have good and strong leaders with a clear vision of what needs to be done. Leaders also show the ability to gather all the energies and get a consensus on the objectives and the path to follow. Unfortunately, all failure stories have leadership in common, too.

Often, such failures are the result of despotic leaders who act more out of self-interest than for the general interest, who work without involving enough of the best people, who do not admit their mistakes and persist in error. In order to succeed and meet food demand by 2050, the world will need leaders, at all levels of society, who have specific qualities. They must have the ability to defuse fears, keep greed under control, address the right issues, foster education, encourage farmers' vocations, be compassionate, work for the general interest, involve and commit all to succeed, and not put their egos first.

To come back to the seven deadly sins analogy, it is just as interesting to see which seven virtues the Roman Catholic Church names. Each virtue is the opposite of one of the deadly sins. The list is temperance, charity, humility, diligence, kindness, patience and chastity. A number of qualities in this list will definitely be useful to succeed in the future.

Since We Cannot Beat Nature...

The saying "*if you cannot beat them, join them*" applies to humanity's dealings with Nature. As a species, humans have been very successful at conquering their environment and exterminating what have threatened and still threatens them. However, the very success that generated the current pace in the increase of human population has created the next challenge. Sustainability is just as much about the population increase as about the use of resources. In 1950, there were "only" 2.5 billion people on Earth. Compared with about seven billion today and the expected nine billion in 2050, it sounds almost like a desert. How does this relate to sustainability? When 2.5 billion people behaved badly, from an environmental point of view, it had consequences, but there was enough room and time for Nature to correct the situation. When seven, or even more so, nine billion people consume and waste precious resources, damage the environment and pollute beyond what is acceptable, the consequences are a lot more serious, a lot faster to appear and require much more determined action to repair. Today, there is significantly less room for error than in the past. As the margin of error per individual has shrunk, the importance of individual responsibility, at home and at work, is much higher than ever before. Today's consumption habits of food as well as non-foods will determine the quality of life in the future.

Sustainability is as much about attitude as it is about production techniques. The natural instinct when facing a problem is to look for the fastest and easiest way of solving it. This preference of the present tends to make the long-term effects of human actions a lesser priority.

Such behavior also tends to ignore how Nature works. Ecology and economy are two sides of the same coin. They are about the dynamics of populations in relation with their environment and the way they can manage the resources that are available to them. The difference is that ecology follows Nature's laws, while economy is a human creation.

The first rule to remember is that Nature simply does not care whether humans exist or not. Nature was there long before us, and it will be there after, too. The calls to "save the planet" are in fact calls to save humanity. Nature is an open field where evolving life forms compete and fill the spaces left available. This is also what humans have done since the beginning of their existence: compete, fight and conquer new habitats.

Nature does not care whether a particular species goes extinct. Only some people do. When a species disappears, others compete to take over the void left, and life goes on. Nature is all about creating balances between species. When a species' population grows fast because of favorable conditions, it always becomes victim of its success. Even insects deplete food resources beyond what could have sustained them. When the food is gone, they simply die by the millions. As far as Nature is concerned, it does not matter if the climate changes, if the nitrate content of drinking water is too high, or if the soil is eroded or contaminated. Let the best species win!

This ability of Nature to adjust constantly to changes in populations of life forms also explains why the efforts to kill threats in agriculture and food production will never be quite successful. While farmers may kill many pests and weeds by using chemicals, pharmaceuticals and genetically engineered crops, they also create a vacuum for other organisms to conquer. This is why antibiotic-resistant bacteria or herbicide-resistant weeds are on the rise. This is simply the result of natural selection and evolution happening right before our eyes.

Resistance was predictable. Individuals with genes that offer a competitive advantage thrive more than the individuals that do not have the resistance genes. Anyone with some biology background knows this fact about mutations and evolution. The history of the use of molecules to fight pests has confirmed that. Some mosquitoes developed a resistance to DDT. The problem of antibiotic resistance has been known for a couple of decades.

That such problems could arise is not a surprise. Changing the environment of species and creating new constant conditions increases the probability of having resistant organisms. The systematic use of large quantities of a particular chemical creates such a constant environment. Organisms mutate constantly and when a trait helps them survive certain farming techniques and products, they thrive. The problem is that it forces humans to find more specific treatment products for the future. This is getting more and more difficult. There is a growing risk that agriculture will have to fight increasingly resistant and strong superbugs, super-bacteria and super-weeds. There are more and more signs that it is the case. Farmers are facing an uphill battle because they are always at least one step behind new mutations and natural selection. It is not impossible for humans to keep the upper hand, though, but the margin of error when looking for solutions will become thinner and thinner. To stay ahead of the game, farmers and all the people involved in food production need to think like ecologists, not just like physicists or chemists. Physics and chemistry, unlike biology, do not deal with living and evolving material. Living organisms are moving targets. This is why repetitive and mechanical methods have limitations. They work with the same statistical effectiveness as the statistical models used to describe biological populations. There is always the standard deviation. There is always the margin of error. There is no absolute and unalterable truth with life. In exact sciences, one plus one always equals two. Biology is a science only statistically exact, and one plus one equals two plus or minus the standard deviation with a certain margin of error.

Because of their contribution to knowledge and to the understanding of how the world functions, science and technology will be the basis for progress. There cannot be any argument against that. What may be arguable is the kind of use humans make of science and technology. Managing ecosystems is one of the underlying principles of sustainability in food production. Humans will succeed only by understanding the big picture and by thinking like chess players. They need to anticipate what the several following moves of the "opponent" will be. To succeed in the fight against pests of all sorts, it is imperative not to give mutations a chance to win. It is essential not to create new stable and "predictable" conditions. If mutations become ineffective, or at least less effective, because the farmers' weapons change regularly, the farmers will win more battles. In sport or in the military, applying the same tactics repeatedly is the surest way to be defeated. It is true for farming, too. Farmers do not even need to exterminate anything. They must manage and contain the enemy. In this game, there is one difference with chess, though. While humans cannot make Nature checkmate, Nature can do that to them.

Nature is quite resilient. If it were not, the consequences of the damages that humans cause, and the imbalances that they create, would have immediate negative consequences. Instead, Nature has the ability to process and repair a lot of damage. People should be thankful for that, because it does not lead to immediate destruction and death. However, it is important to realize that these repairs and processing abilities have limits. Human activities need to remain within the limits and everything will be fine. The secret ingredient to succeed in this strategy is long-term responsible thinking, even if this goes against the short-term interests of some stakeholders. Humans can choose to act like locusts on farmland and consume as much as they can today without thinking of tomorrow. They will have the same fate as the locusts when these eat the last blade of grass available.

Over time, humanity, especially in affluent countries, developed the tendency to forget that Nature's laws are different from human laws. Humans did not make the laws of Nature.

They cannot bend them, either. Religions also emphasize the difference between God's laws and man-made laws, and they discuss which ones should prevail. It is an interesting dimension to bring to the discussion. Although it seems that people see themselves more and more as legal entities before biological entities, their biological nature will prevail, and so will the laws of Nature. The status of legal entity is only useful in the interaction with other humans. Having rights is the result of civilization. Duties come together with rights. Duties are what keep civilization alive. Philosophy, religion, politics, sociology and biology have all contributed to create better and better-functioning societies. Nature's laws do not find their origin in thinking, which is a specifically human trait. Human laws are in constant evolution. They vary between countries, cultures and religions. They reflect the dynamics of societies and the balance of power between different points of views. Nature's laws are not about rights. They are about balance and natural order. In nature, only the species that do not disturb the balance of their ecosystems beyond the point of no return earn the right to survive. It is also useful to realize that not everything that is legal is ethical. Ethics are essential to have a civilized society. They are not about science. Ethics are in the domain of the philosophical, the spiritual and the religious.

"The Lorax" by Dr. Seuss gives a good representation of the debate between industrialists and environmentalists. Although the book was first published in 1971, the story has not aged. The same arguments on both sides are still very similar as four decades ago. There is no shortage of points of views, and the fight is in full swing in all areas of the economy. Interest groups with their own specific agendas are all working hard to influence the rules by which societies function. Interest groups are a good illustration of this shift to legal entities. The fight is about rights. It is about the right to protect people, to protect the environment, or the right to protect the freedom of doing something. The rhetoric is very much the same as the rhetoric that can be heard in courts of law. After all, interest groups and lobbies hire many lawyers.

The art of deciphering the messages from these groups is as much in what they communicate as it is in what they do not mention. There is a lot of information in silence, in omissions and in the phrasing. There is more information in double negatives as there is in straightforward statements. A typical defense argument is that there is no proven evidence that something may be harmful. It is always presented as if it proved that the particular something is harmless. That is not so. The approach is the same as defense lawyers who try to create enough doubt in the minds of the jury members, so that they will not be able to conclude that there is certainty of guilt. Everyone is innocent until proven guilty. The key word is "proven". Not being proven guilty is not the same as being innocent, though. Guilty criminals have been released for this reason. In all things political, there is a simple rule: make the opponent look bad. This is the best way to look a little bit better, which is different than looking good, though. In food and agriculture, a favorite argument is science. All groups have their own facts and science to substantiate their arguments. Of course, the facts are only the convenient facts. Each side claims that the opponents' facts are incomplete, deceiving or manipulative. Similarly, they mention only scientific results that suit their own message. Science has become subordinate to the dogma. Each side claims that the opponents' science is pseudo-science. It is increasingly difficult to find true independent science. Many sponsors, and usually fund providers, are not looking for the absolute science. They just want to set up some research only to prove their point of view. Should it fail to do so, the results will not be published. In the first paragraph of a report, it is easy to identify who may have paid for the research. Usually, the wording tells it all. The same thing that happens in science also happens with media. Depending on who owns the media, and on who reads, watches or listens, the message is adjusted to please the patrons. This way of trying to convince is very human in nature. People fight for what they believe in. They fight for their jobs. They fight for their aspirations. In these ideological debates, nobody has the monopoly of intelligence, knowledge, ethics or morals.

Thinking otherwise is a delusion, and a bit arrogant, too. There are people with much practical experience on both sides of the debate. They have been in the same schools and they have obtained the same degrees. They just have different ideas of how the world should function. The partisan fights can sometimes take an ironic turn, though. When the oil spill in the Gulf of Mexico happened in 2010, it was interesting to hear some of the comments of seafood producers' representatives. They were rightfully outraged by what happened. They found that the oil industry had too much latitude to operate the way it wants, and they were demanding stricter regulations for the oil industry. Their arguments and demands sounded very much like those of environmental organizations, the same organizations that the seafood industry resents so much because of the opposition they offer, as they find that the seafood industry has too much latitude to do what it wants and they wish there were stricter regulations. The grass is always greener somewhere else.

The sad part is that science is gradually becoming suspect. There are now also anti-science groups. Debate is always healthy. Actually, it is healthy only when the debate occurs face to face. Nobody can be right all the time and nobody can be wrong all the time. Nothing is completely black or completely white, either. There is no controversy about the obvious. What is not controversial does not seem to make the news, and non-controversial organizations do not seem to need much PR. Controversies would not last long if the arguments did not have some merit, and they will last until the truth comes out, or when one of the parties involved in the dispute gives up. When an issue requires more understanding and explanations, one must wonder what the most responsible choice is between being cautious or taking chances. Partisan science may seem like a good investment in the short term, but in the long term, it is mostly wasted money. Science that is based on biased assumptions never delivers complete knowledge.

The purpose of true science is not to back arguments. It is to explain how things work, regardless of whether or not the result is pleasant.

Science brings facts to light. Politicians and lawyers twist facts. Science delivers knowledge and understanding of the world. It influences new and better solutions. Humanity has been able to survive because of its ability to understand the world. Stopping pure research is not just delusion, it weakens the ability of humanity to solve future problems. It may hinder the chances of survival. If independent science is becoming rarer, partisan science may still be useful for those with a critical mind who have the willingness to bring together all the pieces of the two puzzles. It might be the only way to get the full picture. Of course, this is an exercise for independent minds. If this work is done by partisan groups, the results might be poor. However, compiling the results of partisan research will always be sub-optimal compared with organized thorough collaboration across the ideologies. Adding partisan science is always a case of one plus one is less than two. Partisan thinking is like using only one eye to see, one ear to hear or one leg to run. It is suboptimal. Using the whole brain instead of only one half is always a smarter choice. Adding all the half-truths that the different parties communicate will never represent the entire truth either. Joining forces would change this formula into one plus one is more than two. Unfortunately, human nature being as it is, the odds of having opponents joining forces are quite low. Crises can change that.

Although science rests on facts, science cannot be the only way to improve. Experience is valuable, too. The modern world tends to consider science to be the only source for progress. If that were the case, humanity would not have made much progress at all. The first farmer who planted a seed in the ground did not know anything about agronomy, but it did not stop agriculture from becoming a major economic activity. Humans did not wait to know about chromosomes, genes and DNA structure to reproduce. If they had waited, the species would have been extinct. In some cases, observation of what works and of what does not work can be at least as effective as science.

It takes time for science to deliver its conclusions and to explain. When choices need to be made fast, the luxury of waiting for the results of science is not always an option.

Science is only a part of the equation. Even the most hardcore proponents of scientific evidence need something else than science to make sense of the world. There is some irony in the fact that many of them will say that they believe in God, for which there is no scientific evidence. It takes more than hard scientific facts to live. Faith, beliefs and ideals are important to have a sense of purpose. The other neglected human asset to make good decisions is common sense. Common sense is the understanding of the outcome of actions through shared experience. Everyone would agree that an open mind is good and that prejudices are bad in a scientific approach, but in many cases, there is no need for scientific reports to know that something may be hazardous. The purpose of the five senses is to inform and warn. Many dangers can be avoided just by listening to common sense. Yet, considering the number of disclaimers about the most obvious dangers with warning about the stupid things not to do, common sense might not be as common and obvious a trait after all. The argument that only scientifically proven facts are acceptable tends to imply that humans should be rational. If they were, they would eat much better and they would not consume excessively all the time. If consumers were rational, they would not have emotions. There would be no joy, happiness or love. There would be no ego. Marketing would simply not work. There would be much fewer consumer products. Many large corporations in the agribusiness, in the food industry, in retail and in foodservice would not exist, or at least would not sell what they offer today. Those who want rational consumers must be careful for what they wish, because they might get it someday. People do not need to be entirely rational as long as they are reasonable and responsible. Next to reason and responsibility, a good dose of pragmatism will be needed to succeed to achieve both meeting future demand and making agriculture sustainable.

Pragmatic Thinking Helps

Although producing food locally makes sense from an intuitive point of view, it is important to look at the issue with an open mind. There is a growing trend, or at least a growing noise in favor of eating locally produced food. Some locavores, as they are called, claim that 100-mile food is the way to a more sustainable agriculture and consumption. Is this approach realistic and could it be the model for the future?

A place where this movement is rather popular is Vancouver, British Columbia, Canada. The laid-back residents who support the local food paradigm certainly love their cup of coffee and their beer. This is a bit of a problem, though. There is no coffee plantation anywhere within one hundred miles. There is not much barley produced around Vancouver, either. Life should be possible without these two beverages, should not it? At least, there is no shortage of water. The disappearance of coffee –and tea- from the households would make the lack of sugar less painful. This is good because sugar beets are not produced in the region, and most of the sugar sold in Vancouver is made from sugarcane, which are produced on the plantations that just happen to be located farther than one hundred miles away. If the absence of coffee and sugar would not be enough, there is no cocoa plantation, either. That would be harsh on the many chocolate lovers. British Columbia does not produce citrus or other warm climate fruit. If Vancouverites are to become locavores, they must say goodbye to orange juice, lemons, pineapples, mangos and bananas. Even the fruit produced in the beautiful Okanagan Valley would not be for Vancouver. The valley rich in orchards where apples, peaches, nectarines and cherries are grown is about 250 miles away. It would not qualify to the locavores.

Even the so popular sushi would disappear because of the lack of rice plantations in the area. It would have to be sashimi instead. There are no rice fields in British Columbia, and neither are there wheat fields. The large local Asian population certainly would have difficulties to eliminate rice from its diet. The lack of wheat means no flour. No flour means no bread, no pastries and no cookies. The carbohydrate supply would be tough. If Vancouverites were to consume all local, their lifestyle would change dramatically. Potatoes and cabbage may be the way of the future. Before going all local food, the locavores must realize that British Columbia produces only 48% of all the food its inhabitants consume. One out of two locavores would have to starve. Going exclusively local would also affect deeply the source of animal protein. Most of the animal feed is made of ingredients that come for much farther than one hundred miles. Animal protein would become less available. Beef ranches are farther away than the 100-mile mark, too. Farmed salmon, British Columbia's largest agricultural export could not use the type of feed they currently use, as fishmeal and fish oil come from Peru and vegetal oil comes from farms located in the Canadian Prairies and in the US Mid-West. Many jobs would be lost with very little alternatives to replace them. The problem goes beyond food. Other agricultural products such as cotton would not be an option anymore. Cars would disappear, because the main component of tires, rubber, is not produced in Canada. The 100-mile rule would solve traffic problems. If local consumption is the rule for food, should it not be the rule for everything as well? China would probably have different views about this. Not only would their manufacturing collapse, but also if they have to produce food within one hundred miles of the consumer, they would have to give up importing agricultural commodities. For them, a true locavore system would mean famine. The same would be true in British Columbia. When people are hungry, they are not so fussy about the distance from the producing farm. The problem with concepts such as the 100-mile diet is that although the basic idea has some value, it quickly evolves into an ideology, and ideologies tend to make their followers stop thinking pragmatically.

Today, the idea of eating locally in a place like Vancouver is possible because supply easily meets demand, thanks to the questionable 3,000-mile foods. If the distance to market has to be within one hundred miles, farmers in low population density areas, such as many regions of North America, South America and Eastern Europe, would have a different type of problem. They would produce an abundance of food, but because there are not enough people to consume it locally, the law of supply and demand would make the price of agricultural commodities plummet, food would stay in storage and farmers would go out of business, while people in China, or in Vancouver, would suffer hunger. Clearly, the 100-mile diet needs some serious amendments.

Intuitively, it sounds logical that locally produced food has a lower carbon footprint than food that comes from 2,000 to 10,000 miles away. However, this is only partly true. The method of transportation affects the carbon footprint. The environmental impact of transport is much higher for road transport than it is for rail transport, which is higher than water transport. The type of transport also depends on the type of commodity brought to market. Perishables need to reach consumers as quickly as possible for shelf life reasons, while dry goods such as grains and oilseeds do not face the same kind of deadline. The quality of the logistics is also crucial to reduce the carbon footprint. A fully loaded truck is much more efficient than a local truck dropping small quantities in many places, thus driving around most of the time with empty space in the trailer. In addition, the argument of the locavores that local has a lower environmental impact can be challenged. Considering the number of SUVs trying to park around Vancouver farmers' markets, that objective might not be achieved as well as intended. Further, many of the Vancouver farmers' market shoppers never miss an opportunity to take a vacation to warm destinations. South California, Arizona, Mexico, Hawaii are among the favorites. They are not exactly within one hundred miles. There are long lines of cars between British Columbia and Washington State because prices for clothes, shoes and alcohol are cheaper in the US. For Vancouverites, there is nothing like a weekend shopping in Seattle, which lies more than one hundred miles away from Vancouver.

The emphasis should not be so much on local as it should be about the search for efficiency and low environmental impact. More than the distance from the farm to the consumer, it would be more useful to provide consumers with information about the actual carbon footprint of the products they buy. They would then have the opportunity to make the right choices. Retailers, too, would be able to make decisions about their sourcing strategies.

Clean products and clean producers need to be rewarded for doing a good job. However, the price of the right products must be more attractive than the wrong ones to conquer market share. In Vancouver, local food products are more expensive than similar offerings from California, Mexico, Ecuador or Chile. Why would families with a tight budget spend more for local products that look pretty much the same? This problem needs to be addressed. Currently, Vancouver farmers' markets are about marketing. They sell the experience as much as their production methods. Only a wealthy minority can afford to buy at these markets. The prices are not based on production costs plus farmers income. They are as high as possible, because the farmers can ask, and get, these prices. Wealthy Vancouverites are willing to pay a substantial premium above what they can buy from the local supermarket. Ironically, they pay premium for fruit and vegetables that present many defects, for which perfectly edible food gets discarded in the regular food supply chain. In this farmer-consumer relation, the price bargaining does not take place. If these farmers were to try to sell to a grocery retail chain, they would never get the prices they get from the consumers who do not haggle about the price. This is why more farmers try to sell directly to consumers: they make more money that way. However, this might change in the future. A number of retailers are working towards offering farmers' market products in their stores. This already makes market farmers nervous.

Another beautiful place where food security sparks debates about local food is Hawaii. Even in paradise, things are not always simple. At the entrance of the Kaloko-Honokohau Historic Park on the Big Island of Hawaii, a sign shows a comparison of the evolution of the food security situation between 300 years ago and today.

By then, there were 150,000 inhabitants on the Big Island of Hawaii. All of the food was produced on the island, and none was imported. They were producing 300,000-500,000 lbs. of fish in stone fishponds. Today, the Big Island population is still 150,000 inhabitants, but only 18% of the food is produced locally. Food imports represent 82%. The Kaloko fishponds do not produce any fish anymore. Of course, the population numbers do not take the number of tourists into account. Moreover, the current food consumption per capita is obviously substantially richer in calories than 300 years ago. There are not many places in the world where the shirt sizes vary from Small to 6XL. That raises some questions about diets that are too rich. In old pictures, Hawaiians used to look slim and had athletic bodies. Clearly, they used to do something right. The example of the Big Island is interesting because it shows that food security depends very much on diet, harmonious relation with Nature and economic interests. If the Hawaiians used to cover their needs with what Nature could offer them, nowadays much of the agricultural land is used for commercial export productions, such as macadamia nuts, coffee and tropical fruit.

In the Historic Park, there were remnants of pits in which rocks were set up in many individual planters. In these planters, called *mala'ai*, the ancient Hawaiians used to grow food plants. This is an ingenious system, because in that area, the fields are covered by lava and are unfit for typical farming practices. There is no soil to be used for open field crops, such as grains, for instance. On the other hand, there would be plenty of acreage to set up such planters. This would be labor intensive, though. Today, the planters are abandoned.

Another ingenious method that Hawaiians had to produce food was the building of fishponds. Aquaculture was a traditional way of improving food security for ancient Hawaiians. The old fishponds were made of walls built with the volcanic rocks, and the fish were passing though gates made of vertical bars. The small fish could enter, but as they grew bigger, they were unable to pass the gates and leave.

As there is a growing opposition to open-net fish farms in many parts of the world, environmentalists claim that land-based closed containment is the only sustainable system. The debate is passionate on both sides and many arguments need to be revisited. The old Hawaiian fishponds are a hybrid form of closed containment. They are actually a quasi-closed containment on the seabed. It does not require all the land-based infrastructure and equipment, as is the case for land-based closed containment systems. The Kaloko fishponds could suggest how the modern could meet the historical and the cultural by developing a responsible and productive aquaculture to increase food self-sufficiency for Hawaii. In a region where the ocean space available is as vast as around Hawaii, there have to be plenty of locations where aquaculture can be conducted without harming the environment, and there have to be more than enough adequate production techniques to do it right. Modern science and ancient wisdom are not mutually exclusive. They complement each other. The partisans of both sides should realize that eventually.

At the Kaimu-Kalapana black sand beach, a sign tells that ancient Hawaiians used to harvest seaweed in a way that was sustainable. It is only after commercial harvesting by European settlers started that the seaweed quantities plummeted because of excessive harvest volumes. Just like for fish production, researchers from all sides should work on restoring seaweed production in a sustainable manner. This example, like all other examples of unsustainable human practices, simply demonstrates that we must produce or harvest what we can, instead of trying to produce or harvest always more while ignoring the signals that we are passing a point of no return.

Many Hawaiian residents express their concern about their dependence on food that comes from far away. Actually, there are more and more conferences and workshops about the topic of food security for Hawaii. Since Hawaii is part of the USA, food security will be guaranteed from the mainland.

However, looking at the situation as if Hawaii was an independent country makes the debate about food dependence from other regions quite interesting. The Islands of the State of Hawaii are isolated, as they lay in the middle of the Pacific Ocean, thousands of miles away from any significant continental mass. If supplies from the continent were to stop, the situation would be dire, and the production techniques of the past would be useful again. They would have to be just improved with modern capabilities.

Just like in most of the rest of the USA, the local food movement is growing. Farmers' markets are gaining in popularity. The food sold on the farmers' markets of the Big Island is quite affordable and actually cheaper than in the large supermarket chains. It is quite a contrast with Vancouver. Not all the food is local, though. At the farmers' markets, many vegetables such as onions, tomatoes or bell peppers were shipped from the West Coast of continental US, mainly Washington State. On the other hand, it is quite interesting to notice that the big national retailers are now selling local products. These retailers will try to be able to source larger volumes, and they actually may be in a position to stimulate more local food, agriculture and aquaculture production.

Is local production for local markets the way of the future? Yes and no. There will be a shift of the location of production for perishables. Consumer habits will change, too. In the West, consumers have been spoiled. They can eat anything from anywhere at any time of the year. This luxury will not be affordable for long anymore. The superfluous will naturally be eliminated.

As the economics of energy, and therefore of food, will change, producers will increasingly locate their operations closer to cities; and even inside cities. Urban farming is a growing activity. Although it started mostly in poor neighborhoods as a way of having a small patch of land for personal consumption, more sophisticated and efficient systems are being developed. Production, and consumption, of vegetables and fragile fruit, for instance strawberries, will gradually become more integrated in the urban landscape than they are now.

Animal productions, such as fresh dairy, poultry meat and eggs are likely to relocate closer to consumer markets, too. The production of non-perishables will not relocate. It does not have to. What will probably change is the transportation infrastructure in many areas where these commodities are produced. This is good news for coffee drinkers and chocolate addicts. After all, transport of commodities over long distance is not just the result of cheap oil. The Silk Road and the spice trade by the Dutch took place before humanity even knew about oil. Trade has always been a force of progress for humanity. It helps an increasing number of people to have access to goods that make their lives better. The rules of trade may not always be fair, but like all human activities, it is a work in progress. Limiting the food supply to one hundred miles would be a regression.

Developing the food systems of the future will need to include many dimensions. One critical element will have to be a broad consensus about how to meet the different points of view. It will happen only if the different stakeholders trust each other about the final objectives.

Regaining the Public's Trust

As society becomes more urbanized, people lose their rural roots. Everyone, directly or indirectly has roots on the countryside. Only two generations ago, the majority of the population in industrialized countries was living in rural areas. In Western countries, the agricultural population represented more than half of the total population. It changed, and the same trend is happening in developing countries. Urbanization, together with modern retail, has created a distance between consumers and farms. People used to know the farmer, the miller, the butcher, the baker and the grocer. The economy was local. Harvests involved many families. Killing the pig was the promise of meat for the months to come. People knew where their food came from. In the modern urbanized world, that connection has been lost. People are physically living away from the farms. This is not just true for consumers. Many executives and employees of agribusiness corporations and their service providers did not grow up on farms, either. If the consumer is disconnected from farms, farmers are also disconnected from consumers. The large corn and soybean farmers do not even produce directly for consumers. They produce for the animal feed industry and, increasingly, for the biofuel industry. It should be no surprise that there is so little mutual understanding between farmers and consumers. The dominant model of intensification, growth, standardization, mass production and mass distribution has led to a restructuring of the entire production and supply chains.

During the past decades, as the economy developed, farmers looked for other jobs in the growing manufacturing sector, and the agricultural population decreased strongly.

In two generations, the agricultural population of Western Europe dropped from 60% to less than 10%, as economic growth offered many jobs in various industries. These jobs also paid better than what small farmers could earn by staying farmers. A similar evolution has been taking place in China since the manufacturing sector developed in the course of the last couple of decades. According to the UN, urbanization will intensify even more. The number of people living in cities will double between 2010 and 2050. In rural areas, the population is expected to decrease by about 25% over the same period. This will happen mostly in Asia and in Africa. In Western countries, the dynamics are different. Populations are aging and they might actually move away from large city centers to find a more bucolic setting. Nonetheless, a decreasing rural population means that farms will become larger on average.

Just as the corporations did, farms grew bigger and bigger. They have reached sizes that have nothing similar with the popular image of the Old MacDonald[2] farm. Then, it is only normal that the same feelings of suspicion appear about agriculture as they did about corporations. As farms were growing in size, consumers started to wonder if they still had the same values. Although the public still trust small farms, the perception of large-scale farms is very different. Small feels human and natural. Big is perceived as impersonal, insensitive and unnatural.

As the consumption society and the modern lifestyle started to show their limitations, Westerners have started questioning the model. They are looking for more balance between professional life and personal life. They are looking for more balance between money, environment and quality of life. Relocation of once secure manufacturing jobs has brought more and more people to question the loyalty of corporations to their employees. Security turned into uncertainty. The emphasis on profit before communities and environment created a fertile ground for criticism.

---

2 From the children's song "Old McDonald Had a Farm". It has nothing to do with the fast food company.

People want the powerful and the rich to care. They want to see reassuring and tangible signs that they actually do. Businesses need to generate profits to continue to operate. Profit always raises suspicions about the intentions of corporations. The size of corporations and the magnitude of profits in times when many people can hardly make ends meet fuel the mistrust. It is human nature. People have already lost faith in politicians. They do not think more highly of the corporate world. This explains the increasing role of the civil society represented by a myriad of non-profit organizations. Already before the economic crisis of 2008, the non-profit sector was a larger employer than businesses. Job opportunities have "relocated". Non-profits, as the name tells it are not about making profits. The negative image of moneymaking does not stand in their way. Moreover, the non-profit sector grew mostly with humanitarian and environmental activities. If they do what they do not to get rich, but for the average people and the little birds, there must be something noble about them. They enjoy the perception of a Robin Hood or of a David defeating Goliath. They have more appeal than the corporations do. The reality is not as black and white as that, though. If companies get their income from their customers, non-profits get theirs from donators. Depending on the organizations, donators may not always be as mundane as one may think. Sometimes, they have political ties with organizations with deep pockets that pursue specific agendas. It can be domestic politics as well as international politics. The world is not always as it seems.

How can agriculture and food regain the trust of consumers? A good way to look at this is to go back to the basics. Regaining trust is much more difficult than earning it in the first place. The baggage will stay in the way for a long time. Therefore, a lot of patience is required. There is no quick fix. Well-crafted video clips and well-thought out press releases are not enough. Trust is not something that can be imposed upon others. It must be earned. Trust is the result of consistent and positive behavior that benefits the other party. People stop trusting when they are disappointed, when they feel betrayed or when they feel unsafe.

By finding out which one of the above caused the loss of trust, and what more specific reasons made the public change their minds, the food sector would already make huge progress. Collateral to this is that the industry needs to do a non-complacent self-criticism. The best way to find out what it would take to regain someone else's trust is to wonder for oneself what it would take to trust again. The empathic exercise is more effective to find out what might work or not. The food sector should do exactly that first, instead of pushing the same message without much success.

Once people have lost trust, they do not believe anything they hear from the distrusted party. In fact, they will hardly listen. Therefore, words alone have little impact, unless they go along with actions that confirm that the message is true. If the food industry does not want to change, and hopes that communication will be enough to change the public's mind, nothing will change. To have proof that someone is reliable, it is essential to see evidence that something is actually changing for the better. The most powerful communication tool that really works to regain trust is non-verbal communication. The distrusted one must sweat to earn back the trust. This does not mean that verbal communication is useless. Verbal communication keeps the relationship alive, but it will not be the critical part for turning around the situation. The superiority of non-verbal communication lies in the fact that it is about actions, while verbal communication is about words. For example, the American meat and poultry sector has undergone many recall procedures due to bacterial contamination over the years, and recalls keep happening. The industry takes measures to solve the problem, because such recalls are very costly. However, as long as there is not a perceptible improvement in the number of recalls, consumers will keep questioning how their meat is produced. Food suppliers have no other choice than to listen to the consumers. The customer is always king. Customers are always right, even when they are wrong. This is business 101. A lot of this is about perception.

For example, in June 2011, Greenpeace published a ranking of Canadian retailers on their seafood procurement, and in particular their sustainability score on seafood. A large retailer organization scored poorly. Its first reaction was to dismiss the assessment made by Greenpeace. However, a few weeks later, it reorganized its seafood assortment from 15 species back to seven sustainably produced seafood species. That is successful non-verbal communication.

Regaining the consumer's trust will require transparency, a lot of patience and communication, and most of all convincing action to meet the market's demand. This does not mean that all consumers' wishes must be met, either. After all, life is a continuous negotiation. There is always some level of compromise between desires and practicality. Reasonable people know and understand that. Food producers and the public need to meet somewhere halfway, but market-driven always trumps production-driven.

It is unclear who the author of the quote *"Tell me and I will forget, show me and I may not remember, involve me and I will understand"*[3] is. It does not really matter. This quote is quite relevant in the debate about agriculture and food. The food sector is under fire on a regular basis. Why does the industry have such difficulties convincing the public? Opponents of agribusiness are very vocal about their opinions. They also show a lot of pictures, documents or footage of what they criticize. They certainly are very active involving as many people as they can. The agriculture and food industry, including aquaculture, also explains a lot and shows some, but not enough about their daily operations. They seem to have a hard time involving enough outsiders of the industry. Industry representatives are wondering why the public is so difficult to convince. After all, the industry claims to have the scientific facts that prove its points. The industry is wondering whether the difference in communication effectiveness is linked to budget amounts or whether it has to do with the quality of the PR officers from both sides.

---

[3] The quote has been attributed to brilliant thinkers such as Confucius, Aristotle, Benjamin Franklin, as well as to some unknown Native American.

It is unlikely that it has much to do with either. It has to do the ability to involve the public with the industry. To involve the public, it is necessary to create an emotional connection first. It appears to be a challenge for the agribusiness. How can farmers and agribusiness connect with people who have little, if any, contact with the agricultural world, and who rarely get to see the reality for themselves? Media and internet are the channels where they find information.

Opponents of agriculture have an easier job in the sense that their first objective is for the current system to change. The worst outcome that can happen to them if they fail is the status quo. They win nothing, but they lose nothing, either. The industry is the one that has the most to lose. Generally, this translates into a defensive approach, and that does not communicate well. Being defensive means having lost the initiative. Only the ones who have the initiative can lead, and only the ones who lead gather followers.

Connecting emotionally means exactly what it says. Rational arguments do not work as long as the connection is not established. The typical response of the food and agriculture sectors is about bringing scientific facts. Such communication is ineffective. Another approach that will fail is "educating" the public. The concept in itself is perceived as incredibly condescending and it creates even more distance. Most people think themselves educated enough, and they certainly do not want to be lectured by those they do not trust in the first place. It is not possible to convince people who do not trust the messenger. Cold scientific explanations will not work. Most people do not have the scientific background to comprehend the so-called scientific facts. Either they will not understand or, worse, they will feel insulted. Such feelings will not help create a strong connection. It will create more distance, which is the problem already.

Anyone who really takes the time to meet and talk with average consumers knows that they are not radical extremists, although some of the activists are. After all, change never comes from conformists. It always comes from people with radical new views.

The average consumer is mostly confused. They get many facts. They get the opposite facts, and they just do not know. Ignorance is not stupidity. Confusing both terms is a major tactical mistake. Average consumers want to know and especially want to be reassured. They are worried about heart disease, diabetes, cancer, food poisoning and allergies. They do not want to get any of them, and they do not want their loved ones to get them, either. That is a normal aspiration. It is not easy for consumers to feel safe when they feel that they do not have options. Food safety issues are not the "privilege" of big agribusiness, though. In 2011, food recalls also happened in the organic sector. The case of the sprouts from Germany, contaminated with the bacteria E. coli, that caused the death of almost 50 people and infected thousands shows that food poisoning can affect any type of food system. The size of operations adds to the magnitude of problems. The meat giant Cargill had to recall 36 million pounds of ground turkey contaminated with the bacteria salmonella Heidelberg during the summer of 2011. The quantity came from only one plant. Expressed in "quarter pounders", a familiar burger size, this quantity would represent 144 million turkey burgers. If this quantity were stored in 40-foot containers, like the ones used for sea shipments, and by aligning all these containers back-to-back, it would create a line of containers of about seven miles long. At about the same time as the Cargill turkey meat recall, strawberries contaminated with E. coli were found at a local farmers' market in Oregon, USA. It is understandable that consumers are worried about food safety. They have a right to explanations. They have the right to feel safe. Food chains, regardless of their concept, have the duty to protect consumers from such dangers.

How can food producers create the needed connection, then? An easy comparison would be the one of the parents who have a child that just had a nightmare. The child's fears are not rational, but they are quite real, as everyone would remember from childhood. Normal parents try to comfort the child. How do they do that?

They ask what the problem is. They listen. They empathize. They tell the child that they will go with the child to the bedroom and show that there is no green monster hiding under the bed. They will lie down on the floor and look under the bed. Then, they will take the child to have a look. They are involving the child. This is how they connect emotionally. It allows them to switch gradually to rational arguments and get the child to go back to bed. Of course, they will not close the door and they will leave a light on so that the child does not feel thrown back at the green monster again. They empathize again. Empathy is their equivalent of corporate social responsibility.

They take good care of those who depend on them. Does anyone seriously think that telling the child that there is no scientific evidence of green monsters would work, or that research has showed that nightmares are not reality? Does anyone seriously think that dismissing the child's fear as unfounded, and therefore stupid, would work? Yet, from a technical point of view, it is pretty much the truth. Of course, it would not work. The child would remain fearful and possibly lose trust in the parents.

If food producers want to regain the public's trust, they will have go look under the bed and peek at it, together with the public. The public could hardly care less for the industry's scientific facts. The public cares about being listened to and about empathy.

PART II

To Feed and Preserve

Many Challenges and Many Opportunities

If it were possible to ask the children of the future what their expectations are about food, it is highly likely that they would name the four following criteria:

- Food security
- Food affordability
- Food safety
- Continuous ability to produce food and to offer all of the above

Since food is essential for survival, nobody looks forward to the prospect of not having any food available. Food means life, and food insecurity potentially means death. The wish to have food security definitely will be on top of the priority list.

Food affordability is also strongly linked to food security or the lack of it. Food insecurity can be the result of the physical lack of food, but it can also be the result of not having the money to buy food. The confusion between the two situations is common, and the apparent answer is to ask for more production. The situation is not that simple, though. It is difficult to imagine that anyone who can afford food would not be able not buy it. If the richest person in the world stayed in the world's poorest village and asked to have a lobster for dinner, someone would undoubtedly figure a way of delivering the delicacy. Food affordability depends on two things: the price of food and the person's income. The price of food is determined by the market, where the law of supply and demand rules. The income depends on many factors, but usually is the reflection of the type of job the person has. Education plays an important role in the level of salary that people can earn. Food affordability depends on the quality of the society.

Food safety is as critical for survival as food security. Supplying contaminated and potentially lethal food is not an option. People should not have to worry about what they eat. A lack of food safety will always result in the demand by consumers to change the food system, because people want to feel safe about what they eat. In order to ensure survival of individuals and stability of the society, food safety is a necessity.

Maintaining the ability to produce enough to feed the population with safe and affordable food is the only way to maintain peace. In order to maintain this ability, food production must be sustainable. Failing to do so will inevitably result in conflicts and human tragedies. They could be minor or major. They could be local or spread to larger regions. The fact that sustainability is time bound brings challenges. The consequences of the way food is produced are not immediate. They may take decades to reach an alarming point. In terms of triple bottom line between profit, people and planet, as it is often described, the reaction times of the three components are very different. It is possible to go online and to follow in real time how much money is in a bank account. Financial results can be checked almost immediately. The social consequences take more time to develop. They can vary from days to decades. Environmental consequences can take even longer to become visible. Ten or 20 years may not be long enough to see the true extent of the damage human activity can cause. The absence of evidence is only absence of evidence, not evidence of absence. Because there is no clear and demonstrable proof of negative consequences, controversies can linger for years, and even decades. However, the truth does not depend on the interpretation of observations. The truth is the truth. It will appear eventually, and humanity will have to deal with it regardless of whether it fits in the preferences or not.

The true discussion is about how many chances humans are willing to take, and what consequences they are ready to accept in the case that they make wrong choices. Because of the long-term effects, sustainability depends on the quality of the leadership, and its ability to manage both short-term and long-term consequences, financially, socially and environmentally.

There is much at stake. Sustainability of food production is about much more than agriculture. It is about a certain choice of society. It is about people's behavior with food and with all resources. It is about their relation with the world.

In a finite environment, it is clear that the maximum average piece of the pie for every person on Earth shrinks when the population grows as it currently does. There will be much less to share when the world's population reaches the expected nine billion by 2050, as there was for the three billion people that populated the planet in 1960. This statement is even truer, as in the course of these 90 years, the quantity of natural resources, such as fossil fuels and metals, will have decreased. Maintaining sustainability with such an increase of population also means that the margin of error per inhabitant decreases. If not enough water is suitable for drinking, if the soils lose their fertility, if the plants and the farm animals are not adapted, if farmers do not have the resources to farm properly, if humans do not know how to manage food production and the environment, then there is a major disaster coming.

With the expected growth of consumption of all goods as the emerging countries grow economically, any waste and any environmental misbehavior will have much stronger consequences than when only 600 million Westerners did. Prosperity and peace will require proper decisions. There will be tough choices to make, and many people will have to accept to be disappointed and frustrated. Their expectations will probably not be met. Unfortunately, if leaders fail to make the right choices, the consequences will be serious. They must make decisions today, or more accurately, they should have made them a couple of decades ago. Time is running out. Procrastination is no longer possible. Critical questions must be answered.

To be able to produce food and meet future demand, it is essential to preserve the Earth's ability to allow a productive agriculture and to ensure that farmers have the means to do the best job they can. Although it may sound mundane, it is useful to look at the basics.

Farmers need good seeds. Having access to plants with good genetic potential and that are adapted to the local conditions is the starting point. If seeds do not meet these criteria, there is no chance that the farmers will be able to produce significant yields. Too many farmers, especially small farmers in Africa or Asia can only buy poor quality seeds that have not even been cleaned, which means that they are mixed with other plants, mostly weeds that undermine yields and add to the workload. Often, these farmers are poor and for them, expensive seeds are not affordable. Their yields are poor, but just by having better seeds and having the ability to buy proper tools and the needed inputs, production would increase very quickly to levels that are much more in line with farms in other regions of the world. For instance, in the case of wheat, yields in Western European countries vary between six and nine tons per hectare. In the USA, the average yield is about three tons per hectare, which is the world average. In Africa, the average yield is about 1.5 ton per hectare. There is no reason why Africa could not be able to reach at least the world average. There are large areas of arable land that are not in production. According the FAO (Food and Agriculture Organization of the United Nations), the area of unexploited arable land in Africa covers 700 million hectares. This is as large 90% of the area of continental USA. This is twice the size of India. If such an area could be developed into efficient agriculture and produce similar yields as in farming regions where farmers have access to the necessary resources to deliver good work, the African continent would become a major agricultural producer and make Africa a net food exporter.

What is needed to succeed is to gather the energies to give the farmers the ability to produce properly. The problems are many, but they revolve around the lack of money and the lack of infrastructure.

None of that is impossible to overcome. There is plenty of money in the world to achieve the transformation. Failing to take action will mean less food, higher food prices and social unrest or worse.

Farmers need fertile land. There are two important parts in this statement. Everything that takes away good arable land from agriculture is simply reducing the quantity of food that farmers can produce. The development of urban areas is a substantial "consumer" of arable land, as most cities are built around water sources and fertile land. Although in many countries, it is theoretically forbidden by law to use arable land for other forms of development, the unacceptable happens. Residential developers have the financial power to "convince" local authorities to grant them land and expel farmers. The development of manufacturing sites is another form of destruction of the potential for adequate food production. For some farmers, this is actually a very interesting situation, as they can get more money for their land to be developed than if they were to sell it as farmland. Such situations are on the rise in countries like China and India, where food security is far from being a given. Here are certainly future cases of their reaping what they sowed. The second part of the statement is about fertility. Having land is one thing, but ensuring that the soil is fertile is another. Human activities have a negative impact on soil fertility. It can be the result of erosion, it can be the result of excessive intensive practices, it can be the result of poorly skilled farmers or it can be the result of pollution and contamination by other activities, such as manufacturing.

Having a fertile soil and good seeds is not enough. Farmers need water, but water is available in limited quantities. If all the water on Earth were gathered in a sphere, this sphere would have a diameter of about 1,400 km. As a comparison, the diameter of the Earth is 12,800 km! Moreover, the quantity of usable fresh water represents only 1% of the world's water, only 1% of the 1,400-km sphere. Agriculture, through irrigation, uses 70% of the world's fresh water. Therefore, practices that help preserve the amount of water available are essential for the sustainability of agriculture. This depends on the local climatic conditions, the local water availability conditions, the local policies, the type of production and the farmers' practices. Clearly, producing crops that require a lot of water in regions where it is scarce will eventually cause problems.

The same is true about exporting water-rich crops away from regions that have scarce reserves. There are also unexploited water reserves. This is especially the case in Africa. The water is there, but the infrastructure is lacking. Helping farmers to have access to water is one of the important actions to help them achieve higher yields.

Besides having enough of good arable land, good seeds and enough water, farmers need to enrich the soil and ensure that plants have enough nutrients. Good management practices are essential, but external changes will affect the price and the sources of fertilizers. The production of chemical nitrogen fertilizers rely largely on the use of natural gas. As the demand for fossil fuels increases, so will the price of nitrogen fertilizers, too. Strategies to reduce losses will become an absolute necessity for the financial viability of farms. The gradual depletion of phosphate mines will also result in higher fertilizer prices. Price increases, although never popular, have one major advantage. They stimulate the search for smarter and more efficient alternatives. When something is cheap, waste is hardly noticeable on the bottom line. When something is expensive, waste matters. Financial efficiency goes along with technical efficiency. Price pressure always stimulates innovation.

To ensure an adequate food production, farmers also have to fight weeds and pests. Plant diseases, insects, worms or fungi can have disastrous effects on yields, and therefore on food supplies. Farmers need to be able to control the pests, and they must keep their ability to do so. Resistance to chemicals is a growing concern, as it leaves farmers with very few, if any, tools to fight the pests. The same problems are true for weeds. It is essential to fight weeds to have good production volumes.

The estimate of worldwide yield losses due to weeds represents a grain equivalent that could cover the nutritional needs of about one billion people. Farmers must be in a position to reduce food losses because of weeds. They must not lose the battle. Of course, there is always the option of manual weeding, but this is labor extensive and expensive. Chemical herbicides have replaced manual labor in many agricultural regions.

The weed resistance to glyphosate currently on the rise is a major source for concern. The chemical industry has had no new herbicide to offer since glyphosate. Glyphosate is the most efficient herbicide, as it can kill almost any plant. The resistance to glyphosate forces farmers to use herbicides that had been developed before glyphosate. These products are less effective, more limited in their scope and environmentally less friendly than glyphosate. The critics of GMOs blame the systematic use of glyphosate on glyphosate-tolerant engineered crops for the weed resistance problem. Could inserting a gene of resistance to the other herbicides, as this is currently in development by the GMO producers cause the same consequences, and then make all chemical herbicides irrelevant? If so, it could bring agriculture back several decades in time. This is certainly an exciting topic for debate.

Regardless of the size of their farms and the production model that farmers choose, they need financing for their operations. Farming is a risky business. Many things can go wrong, and to prevent them from happening, farmers must have access to all the relevant tools that they need. Money is critical to keep farms, and thus food supplies, alive. Farmers must have enough access to cash to provide the world with enough food. According to the FAO, about 70% of the billion people hungry on Earth are small farmers and their families. They are poor. They do not have access to what they need to succeed. Food supply needs farmers. Agriculture needs to attract people by showing that it can be a viable living.

To ensure sustainability of adequate food production volumes, one variable is still out of the farmers' control. It has been so since the dawn of agriculture. It is often unpredictable and it may affect the future of humanity: the climate.

As climatic change is a very gradual process, it is understandable that not everybody agrees on what is happening and what may happen in the future. Dealing with the climate change issue is really about taking a long-term approach by assessing risk and taking adequate measures.

It is impossible to predict with certainty any event, but there are many clues that indicate that preventive, as well as corrective, actions are necessary. In the debate, there are four main groups. There are the people who believe that the climate is changing. There are those who do not think it is happening. There are those who think climate change is real but it is not the result of human activity. Finally, there are those whose objective is to create doubt simply because they do not want to change. For them what will happen in 50 years from now does not matter. They have short-term interests to preserve.

All that scientists can present are projections based on assumptions. There is no possibility to confirm with absolute certainty the accuracy of any assumption. The only way to find out would be to do nothing and wait. If the pessimistic scenarios are correct, doing nothing will end in disaster. Climate change is really a risk management exercise. It is a choice between caution and risk taking. Extreme climatic events happen, but they do not follow any consistent pattern, and they have happened in the past, too. It is easy for skeptics to claim that nothing serious is really happening. Climate change will not really affect the current deciders who are middle-aged at best. The ones who will suffer are the young people born today and the children that they will have.

The deniers are easy to identify. So is their agenda. The consensus of the scientific community does not share their views. Although there is room to deny any link between climatic events and climate change, the number of these events and their frequency are reasons for concern. It is not possible, in all intellectual honesty, to say with absolute certainty that climate is not changing. There have been many extreme events, such as the floods in Pakistan and South Asia in 2011. The tornadoes that hit the USA during the spring of 2011, killing more than 500 Americans, and that happened again in 2012 should be reason for perplexity. The shift of the jet stream that caused frigid temperatures in usually warm areas such as Arizona, while causing unseen warm temperatures in usually frigid places such as Chicago in the spring of 2012 is puzzling.

The droughts in Russia in 2010 that ignited the strong increase of the price of agricultural commodities, followed by the droughts in China and France in 2011 should make everybody wonder about what might come in the future if climate change is real. The list of problems and their consequences can neither be ignored nor dismissed. True leaders cannot reject the hypothesis that climate change might be causing such events. The magnitude of recent climatic events may hint towards ones that are more serious. Nobody can know if the world is due to face problems of biblical proportions, but the story of the plagues of Egypt comes to mind.

The Pharaoh was defiant of Moses' threats. Even after seeing the water become unfit for consumption, the explosion of the population of pests, the surge of diseases on people and livestock, violent climatic events destroying crops, the Pharaoh was still not quite convinced. His advisors and magicians were claiming that it was only magic as they replicated a number of Moses' actions. To accept reality, the Pharaoh had to see his first-born die. Of course, this story is only a story, but it illustrates some basic human reactions when facing events that are difficult to explain and that challenge the present order of power and influence. Will the world leaders allow more problems to happen? Will it take the death of some of their dearest relatives to show adequate political will to change? The future will tell.

Opposite to the skeptics who never provide any proof that climate change is not happening, many serious organizations express their concern about climate change. The US Department of Defense published a report stating that climate change is a major threat to the national safety of the USA. The Pentagon is not exactly a tree hugger organization. Ironically, the lobbies that contest climate change and try to undermine action against it have political affinities with the military lobby. Other serious and well-recognized organizations, such as the FAO and the IEA publish many warnings about the risks of climate change. In the World Energy Outlook 2011, the IEA expresses concerns about the risk of reaching a temperature increase of 2°C compared with the pre-industrial era, which would bring climate change to an irreversible phase.

They clearly state that postponing action is not economically sensible. For every dollar of investment that would be delayed before 2020 in the energy sector, the cost to compensate for the emissions that would result from that lack of investment will be 4.3 times higher after 2020! The main risk is procrastination. Energy demand will keep rising strongly, but the world can cope with it, according to the IEA. However, it can happen only if governments take timely proper actions.

The reason behind the resistance and the denial of climate change is actually very mundane. It is about money. Climate change is an incremental process. It takes years to show significant effects. Opposite to this, the effect of tougher legislation is immediate. The negative impact on costs and on jobs manifests quickly. The negative short-term impact is even more sensitive in a time of economic hardship. In such conditions, it becomes more difficult to gain acceptance for long-term sacrifices while there is no viable alternative to generate at least an equivalent profit and employment in the short term. Of course, subsidies can alleviate the pain and make the transition acceptable, but they are difficult to justify in times when government deficits take alarming proportions everywhere around the world.

The path of least resistance and the preference of the short-term prevail. The leaders choose not to be courageous. Such a conclusion is common, and it is a simplistic one. Is the failure to take courageous decisions only the responsibility of the leaders? To answer this question, one must wonder how many people in polluting industries would accept to sacrifice their jobs, their livelihoods to save the next generation. If there is no viable alternative, the answer will be a loud "No!" without the shadow of a doubt. Similarly, one can wonder if consumers would be willing to stop buying products that contribute to climate change. Would they give up their cars and switch to bicycles? Unless the alternative would be much more painful, it is likely that they would answer "No!" to that question, too. In the current economic model based on consumption, asking people to cut back on consumer goods to live lives that are more frugal would cause a deep recession.

Such a proposal will never receive the support of the political and business deciders, even if it would keep the world livable for the coming generations. The truth is that everybody is responsible for the problem, not just the leaders. Everybody enjoys the convenience and the comfort created by mass consumption. Very few would be willing to give it up voluntarily. The lack of political will, as it is called, showed by the world leaders is only a reflection of the collective inertia. While many people are contributing to the problem, nobody feels responsible for it. It is always someone else's fault. Climate change can be seen as an illustration of Jean Paul Sartre's quote *"Hell is other people"*. It is difficult to hope to see a solution to the problem as long as nobody is willing to acknowledge responsibility and take action so drastic that others will feel compelled to follow the example. The world leaders skillfully dodge their opportunity to state whether they think climate change is a problem or not. It would be nice to hear from the different countries how they feel about the issue. It would also make it easier to understand why they act the way they do. Climate change is a problem or it is not a problem. The leaders who think that climate change is not a problem should say so. Those who think it is should do the same. Of course, those who would state that it is a problem will have to develop their plan to show what they want to do about it.

Failure to do so would look strange. Another reason why talks about climate change make so little progress is the lack of vision for the future. The international conferences try to address greenhouse gases emissions without addressing the economic model of the consumption society at the same time. In such a model, where people are supposed to buy more and more goods that are cheaper and cheaper, that are made and delivered with massive amounts of energy and natural resources, there is simply no climate-friendly alternative. There will probably never be any climate-friendly alternative in the future, either. There is no point in being hypocritical and in trying to make believe that the economy can grow forever. It is not possible to increase the use of finite resources in a finite system indefinitely. It is physically impossible, but it is possible to deny it.

In this case, humanity will reap what it will have sowed. However, it is possible to debate and find out where the point of no return is. Even if some countries have higher emissions than others do, pointing fingers at them is not productive. Greenhouse gases emissions may be produced locally, but their effects extend much farther than the national borders. The solutions must be global and developed by all countries as a team. They need to have a vision and a plan to reduce the effects globally. As different sources of energy have different effects on the level of greenhouse gases emitted, the focus should be more on how to produce the required energy than on where the problem originates. The conferences should offer brainstorming sessions about solutions and concrete funding measures for cleaner energy production. The approach should be one of a global contest to offer systems that solve the problem. It would be interesting to change the discussion from one focusing on by how much which country should reduce greenhouse gases emissions into one focusing on developing a vision for energy production, both quantitative as qualitative. The next step is how to produce the amount of energy needed in the future while producing this energy below a global limit that all parties must define. Since money plays a central role in political decisions, it could be a good idea to organize a different type of conference. This time, the participants would have to present all the scenarios that would be possible if they did not consider the short-term economic consequences. It would be stimulating to hear how the problem can be solved from a technical point of view. The solutions would have to review all the possibilities for all industries, starting by the most polluting, to produce more with fewer emissions. Once this part would be completed, the next question would have to address how much these scenarios would cost, and to elaborate a plan that would fund the winning solutions. Nowadays, economic decisions seem to be based on the *too-big-to-fail-bailout* concept. Then, why not apply the same approach to humanity and climate? Pumping as much money as necessary to ensure the transition in order to create the energy production of the future and save humanity from much costlier consequences sounds reasonable. It would be interesting to compare it with the amount of money printed and the amount of debt created to alleviate the effect of the Great

Recession of 2008 that still lingers in many regions today. Unfortunately, the money already printed is no longer available, and this limits the amount that governments could make available in the future.

While the economic model is flawed and needs to be altered to the future demographic and economic situation, it will not be easy to change. The current model is the only one that has been in use for decades, or even since the second half of the 19th century, when the Industrial Revolution began. Modern agriculture has followed a pattern that fits in the Industrial Revolution and consumption society models. To adapt the economy to the future and ensure the sustainability of humanity, it is necessary to change the economic model. If producing goods for mass consumption is not the future, which model will be able to replace it? The question really comes down to finding an alternative model that provides prosperity. The new model must offer the possibility for all people to make a proper living and to be able to cover their needs. It is necessary to unlearn the current model, and to look at the economy from the human needs point of view instead of looking at it from the industrial production potential. It can be done.

Like any other human activity, agriculture contributes to the emission of greenhouse gases. The exact percentage of greenhouse gases produced by agriculture is still unclear. There are many different numbers presented. The gases originate from fertilized soils, enteric fermentation, biomass burning, rice production, as well as manure and fertilizer production. Agriculture is a major part of the world economy.

Depending on the choices that the leaders will make for future generations, the consequences will affect food production, too. Even if the main culprits of greenhouse gases emission are from various industries, the consequences will appear everywhere.

The projections show that tropical and sub-tropical regions are likely to suffer the most from an increase of temperatures. In regions with a dry season, agricultural output could drop significantly both for vegetal and animal productions.

Some predictions indicate strong drops in yields. The reasons are many. They vary from higher temperatures, desertification, salinity and water shortages. However, it is important to look at such forecasts cautiously, because in many cases, the current agricultural output in these regions are far from being at the level that they should be if farmers had access to good seeds and proper tools, inputs and money to produce efficiently. If they only had the ability to have access to proper modern technology, and this does not mean using all the latest hi-tech tools, the yields would be much higher. If In Africa, where agriculture produces far below potential, the local farmers could just reach yields at the world average level, which is possible from a technical point of view, even a drop in yields in a few decades from now, would still mean a substantially higher agricultural production than at the beginning of the 21st century. The prediction of yields variation due to climate change always seems to assume that farmers would produce the same crops in the same places. It does not have to be true. As climate changes, it is only natural to expect the geographic distribution of crops to change, too. Some crops may see their yields decrease, but other crops might do better. For instance, cassava yields would likely increase if the climate of Africa becomes warmer.

If tropical and sub-tropical regions are expected to suffer from a warmer climate, it is quite possible to foresee that cold regions might benefit from a rise of temperature. This part seems to be always neglected in future scenarios. The two largest countries on Earth, Russia and Canada, would have serious potential to produce more. Higher temperatures would help increasing yields, and would allow more acreage to be in production.

It would be interesting to estimate what an increase of temperature of 2 or 3 degrees Celsius would represent in terms of additional agricultural production in these two countries. If the ice cap that covers Greenland melts away, the small Kingdom of Denmark may become one of the largest habitable countries in the world. Against such a potential upside, it is necessary to consider that the rise in sea level predicted by the scientists means a loss of land. Flat coastal regions, deltas, islands and archipelagos will be threatened.

For instance, Bangladesh will be submerged. The country is the seventh most populated country on Earth, with a population density of almost 1,000 people per square kilometer. This is a density more than 2.5 times as high as India's and about 30 times that of the USA! The rise in sea level will have major consequences, not only for Bangladesh, but also for the entire Indian subcontinent and for all of South East Asia. There are major delta areas that produce large amounts of rice in that part of the world. This is the case of Pakistan, the sixth most populated country in the world, and Vietnam, the 13th most populated country. There are many islands, too. Indonesia, world's fourth most populated country and the Philippines, number 12 on the list, are countries that consist of islands. Undoubtedly, they will suffer direct consequences from climate change. All countries with a coastline would be affected, not only in developing countries. Wall Street would be under water. Miami would disappear.

The forecasters must be careful not to mix current problems that originate from lack of infrastructure and poor political management with the problems that will result directly from climate change. Projections about the consequences of climate change on future food production tend to focus too much on regions that have difficulties today. It is legitimate to focus on these regions, but for the future, it is necessary to look at the complete picture. It is necessary to foresee how each region in the world will be affected and to quantify the changes for food production levels. How much arable land will appear or disappear and what will the yields be?

The consequences of climate change needs to be looked at in a dynamic manner and in terms of survival strategies. This will give a better idea of what may happen in the future. There are many challenges ahead, but there are also many possibilities to improve production volumes in the meantime. The balance is not just about doomsday scenarios. Future recommendations need to warn against problems, but they also must uncover the areas for hope. Despair is not a good motivator.

We Will Reap What We Sow

A Complex Multi-level Issue

Answering the question of how many people the world can feed is more complex than it may sound at first. It depends on many factors, a number of which have nothing to do with agricultural production.

In 2012, there are just above seven billion people on Earth. The one billion hungry people would tend to indicate that there is a shortage of production of about 14%. However, also about one billion people on Earth are overweight and obese. In many countries, not just in Western countries, the daily average intake of calories exceeds the nutritional needs. In terms of calories, the two groups, the hungry and the fat, tend to balance each other. The rest of the population, about five billion people, is fed "reasonably". On average, today's food supply easily covers the calorie requirements of all seven billion. Clearly, the problem is that some can buy and consume much more than they need, while others cannot buy enough food.

However, the current consumption does not tell the whole story. Large volumes of food are wasted. According to the FAO, 30% to 40% of all foods produced are not eaten. Either food is thrown away at the household, retail and restaurant level, or it is lost before it can reach the market, also referred to as post-harvest losses.

The first kind of waste is mostly typical of rich countries. The tonnage of food thrown away by consumers in rich countries is almost as high as the total food production in sub-Saharan Africa. Unfortunately, a similar behavior seems to emerge in the wealthier layer of society in emerging countries, too. Human nature is rather universal, and bad behavior knows no borders.

The government of India is considering implementing a fine to those who waste food. In a country where 200 million people do not have enough to eat, food waste is indeed unacceptable, and even more so when it is the result of complacency and selfishness. When food becomes relatively cheap in comparison to income, it seems to be taken for granted. The reverse is also true. Since the beginning of the economic crisis that started in 2008, many more initiatives have been taken in rich countries to reduce waste and serve the most vulnerable with food that is discarded by supermarkets or restaurants. Non-profit organizations are collecting food in cooperation with business owners to be able to offer fresh and safe food to the hungry. Businesses also actively look for solutions to save food from going to the landfill. For instance, Wal-Mart, the world's largest retailer, has set up the proper infrastructure to offer perishables to food banks, among others. Improvement in logistics was necessary because the supply chain for perishables to food banks was absent. When food becomes more precious, people find ways to save it from being wasted.

Logistics and infrastructure are also the weak links to bring food to consumption markets in developing countries. They are the main causes of post-harvest losses. The tragedy in this situation is that the food has been produced. It is edible and ready to be consumed. Unfortunately, the storage and transport are deficient, and the food is lost because it rots in poor storage conditions or even on the fields. It is contaminated with mold or spoilt or it is eaten by vermin.

Not only are post-harvest losses a waste of food, but they are also a waste of all necessary inputs to produce the food, such as water, seeds, energy, fertilizer, the farmer's money and time.

For these reasons, post-harvest losses have negative effects financially, socially and environmentally. Post-harvest losses represent 20% of all the food produced in the world, according to FAO's estimates. This number represents huge quantities of food. Preventing the post-harvest losses can dramatically change the food security situation of some countries.

In China, the quantity of wheat that is lost between the farm and the market is estimated at the volume that Canada exports and Canada is the world's second exporter of wheat. Clearly, the current situation weighs negatively on the price of wheat. In India, the estimate for post-harvest losses also reaches high numbers. This is especially true for produce, for which the losses can reach as high as 50% of the total production.

To see the impact of post-harvest losses, a simple calculation is useful. According to the World Bank, the world agricultural GDP[4] for 2010 is estimated at US$3.6 trillion. Assuming that the food lost post-harvest has a value comparable with the average of all the foods included in the world agricultural GDP, the value of all foods, including post-harvest losses would amount:

US$3.6 trillion/80% = US$4.5 trillion

The theoretical value of the post-harvest losses can be estimated at:

US$4.5 trillion– US$3.6 trillion = US$900 billion

Of course, this is a theoretical calculation and the assumptions can be disputed. However, even in the extreme case that the assumption would be so wrong that the result would be only a tenth of what the above calculation shows, the value of post-harvest losses would still amount to US$90 billion. The calculation becomes particularly interesting when it is compared with the estimate of the cost to fix the infrastructure deficiencies. The FAO estimated this cost at US$83 billion by late 2011. The payback time for the investments in infrastructure to solve post-harvest losses would then be less than a year! Yet, infrastructure improvement is happening only very slowly. Part of the problem is that nobody can fix it all alone, and the solution requires leadership and cooperation between all parties involved.

---

[4] GDP: Gross Domestic Product, is the total of the market value of all goods and services produced within a country.

The issue of post-harvest losses is an interesting case, as it covers many areas, and it shows how many players would benefit from a collaborative approach. The farmers would benefit because, instead of losing their production, they would be paid for it. In many developing countries, governments pay subsidies to farmers to produce more food, and they also subsidize food for low-income families. Production subsidies end up being for nothing when the food is lost. With no losses, there would be more food on the market. This would reduce inflationary pressure on the price of food for the public, and therefore, food would be more affordable. More affordable food would mean that less money would be needed to subsidize low-income families as well. As post-harvest losses would be eliminated, the government money spent in subsidies would be used more efficiently, and the total amount of subsidies would be lower. This is a financial advantage for the government, but there is also a social advantage. As food would become more affordable to more people, the risk of social unrest would decrease. Solving the post-harvest loss problem will contribute to more social stability in developing countries. Wholesalers and retailers would also benefit, as more affordable food would increase the volumes of food that they would sell. Storage companies, installation and maintenance companies and transporters would all benefit from increased business activity. All businesses involved in the value chain and the supply chain from farm to consumer would have more activity.

Employment would also increase, as more business activity would require more employees to deal with the extra volumes of food brought to market. Better employment also means fewer social issues for the government to solve, more satisfaction for the population and theoretically more support from the population to the countries' leaders. In this picture, there are no losers, only winners.

A quick calculation shows how many people all the lost food, post-harvest and consumer waste, could and should have fed. By keeping the billion hungry people apart, it is fair to say that the world currently feeds reasonably or more than reasonably a total number of six billion people.

By setting food waste at 30%, these six billion people eat only 70% of the actual world production. The number of people that the food actually produced can feed is six billion divided by 70%, or 8.5 billion people. By adding the amount of calories consumed by the one billion hungry, and the amount of excessive calories consumed by the overweight and the obese, it is fair to say that the current food production already covers the needs in calories of nine billion people.

Although the previous calculation is theoretical to some extent, it is reassuring to realize that the world produces already enough food in 2010 to cover the needs for calories required by the expected population of 2050. The issue of waste is not about agricultural technology. It is about organization and behavior. It is about leadership and action. Eliminating waste is only a matter of willingness to do so. The money is there and the technology is there. All it will take to succeed is to decide to do it. Solving the food waste issue or not will depend on everyone. It is really a case of reaping what has been sowed.

However, feeding the future world's population will depend on other factors, too. It will depend on what products the people of the future will demand, and what their diet will be. A clear trend is the higher demand for animal protein. The production of 1 kg of animal protein, be it meat, eggs or milk, requires more than 1 kg of grains and oil seeds. This is the challenge.

As consumption of animal protein increases, the demand for vegetal commodities will increase much more than it would have if people had consumed limited amounts of animal protein. To produce more grains and oilseeds requires the increase of two factors: the acreage in cultivation and the yields.

With the increase of the population and economic development, the area of available arable land shrinks. Good land is covered with cities, roads, industrial estates and residential development. Although in many countries the law says that agricultural land must be used for agriculture only, corruption often trumps the law.

For instance in China, many farmers are expelled from their land to allow residential developers with connections to build on good arable land, or for industrials to build manufacturing plants. China has a serious food security problem. Yet, they seem to continue to lose arable land to other activities, as well as they are slowly running out of proper water for food production and lose large amounts of soil because of wind erosion, in a similar way to what happened in the notorious "Dust Bowl" of the USA during the Great Depression. By allowing these problems to continue and become bigger, China may jeopardize its future social stability. In India, there are also many cases of farmers who prefer to sell their land to developers, because they can get much more money per acre than they would if they sold their land to other farmers for the purpose of agriculture. India is another country with a serious food security problem. If they choose to lose good land for other purposes and sacrifice food production, they must realize that they will face their karma.

If agriculture loses arable land for some good reasons and for some less glorious ones, there are more areas to develop. Even countries that play a major role in food production have potential to produce more. Brazil is one example. According to the FAO, Brazilian agricultural production can increase by 40% during the decade 2011-2020. Similarly, huge progress is possible in Russia, Ukraine and Kazakhstan through better organization, agricultural development and infrastructure improvement.

Regardless of the evolution of the acreage available for agriculture, a key factor for food security, as well as for the profitability of a farm, is the yield. The more farmers can produce per hectare, the better their revenue is. In some areas the potential for improvement may be better than in others, but yields can be improved everywhere.

Between regions, yields for a same type of crop vary, sometimes largely. For wheat, farmers in Western Europe achieve yields varying from about 6 tons/hectare to 9 tons/hectare. In the USA, the average yield is around 3 tons/hectare.

The other large exporters, such as Canada, Ukraine, Argentina, Russia, or Australia, yields are even lower. They fluctuate between 1.5 and 2.5 tons/hectare. In Africa, yields vary between countries, but on average, the yields are around 1.5 ton per hectare. In the case of corn, the variation is similar. American and French farmers achieve yields on average in the order of 9 to 10 tons/hectare. This is especially interesting because American farmers use GMO plants and the French do not. Yet, their yields are similar[5]. In Argentina, another large corn producer, average yields are in the range of 6 to 8 tons/hectare. In Brazil, corn producers hardly reach 4 tons/hectare on average. In the Netherlands, yearly averages have reached 13.5 tons/hectare. All these numbers are averages. It means that the best farmers reach even higher yields. Clearly, such variations show that the limiting factor for production is not as much the genetic potential as the conditions of production.

Yields that are below genetic potential are not just for vegetal productions. The same is true for animal husbandry. During InnoVision 2009, organized by the Dutch company Nutreco, Dr. Leo Den Hartog, Professor Animal Production at Wageningen University, stated that farm animals produce at 30% to 40% below their genetic potential. There is room to produce more efficiently in animal production, too.

The technical performance of Western European farmers is among the best in the world and many countries should try to meet their performance. Their potential for improvement is lower than it is in other regions. Clearly, the highest potential to increase production is in countries that have the lower yields. This is especially true for countries where the low performance is the result of lagging development, poor infrastructure and deficient organization.

---

[5] There are many statements of all sorts about GMOs, but for some reason, yields comparisons and evolution of yields over time seem to be missing from discussions. However, stats are available. See the graph about corn yields in Appendix 2.

Since yields are the expression of the interaction between the genetic potential of the plants with the effects of the environment, variations give an idea of how much more farmers could produce if they could control and manage the environment better.

Many factors play a role: temperature, precipitation, amount of sunlight, soil quality and fertility, fertilization, weeds, pests and diseases. This is not the entire list, though. Under environmental factors, the list must not be limited to natural conditions. Farmers are an integral part of the environment. The skillfulness of farmers plays an essential role. Even within a region, yields vary, sometimes with large differences between farmers. Agriculture is not different from other economic sectors. Some farmers perform simply better. They have a better understanding of their field, they have a natural talent, they are better trained, they are better informed about production techniques or they are more driven than others are. Education and training, together with high quality technical support is essential to increase agricultural production everywhere in the world. Another crucial part of the farming environment is access to sufficient financial resources. Achieving adequate production requires money, simply to have access to all the necessary inputs and tools. Many farmers, especially in developing countries, do not produce enough because they live in poverty. They cannot buy good and clean seeds. They cannot buy fertilizer or cannot mechanize some of the heavy-duty tasks because they do not have the money, and because nobody wants to lend to them. In many cases, the amounts of money needed are not even high, but they would be sufficient for these farmers to do a better job.

They know how to farm, and because of their precarious situation, they are already resourceful and creative to produce as efficiently as they can, considering the circumstances. This vicious circle is difficult to break without external help. This is why about 70% of the world's hungry happen to be small farmers. They produce food, but not enough to feed themselves. If they can get the support to farm properly, they will boost their production, they will improve their incomes, and many more might have enough to feed themselves, their families and their local communities.

Africa is the only continent where agriculture has hardly made any progress over the last few decades. There, yields have actually decreased over time. It is the result of poor leadership, corruption, poverty and deficient infrastructure. The lack of development is extreme in some cases. For instance, according to estimates, 90% of the arable land in the Republic of Congo is unexploited. This is even more dramatic as Congo is one of the countries where people have the lowest calorie intake, of about 1,600 calories per day. To simplify and get an idea of the potential of Africa, a calculation in wheat equivalent gives an indication. It could be possible to use cassava for the calculation, but wheat is produced in more regions and it offers more possibilities for comparing yields. With the assumption that wheat yields would be the same as the current African average, a low 1.5 tons per hectare, the additional acreage would add up to 1.05 billion tons of wheat (700 million hectares of unexploited arable land times 1.5 ton per hectare). There are about 3,000 calories in a kg of wheat. Since an average human being needs about 660,000 calories per year, one ton of wheat can feed about 4.5 people. From a calorie point of view, the 1.05 billion tons of wheat can feed 4.7 billion people.

The number would be less if a part of the wheat equivalent is used to feed animals for the production of animal protein. The potential of Africa could rather easily contribute to feed between 1.5 and 2 billion more people in the world than today's world agricultural production can.

There is no reason to think that African farmers could not match the performance of farmers elsewhere if they have access to good seeds and inputs like their Western counterparts. If they get the means to succeed, they will succeed. There is no reason why African farmers could not double, triple or even quadruple the yields of their crops within a couple of decades. A doubling of yields would feed twice as many people as the previous calculation indicates. Clearly, this performance can be achieved with traditional techniques and good quality seeds. This is not even about high-tech or GMOs. Within two generations or maybe even less, Africa has the potential to become a net exporter of food. Many Asian countries and Arab countries have seen this potential.

This is why they purchase large areas of land over there to develop agriculture. These countries have large amounts of cash available to develop production, but they all lack land within their own borders. Africa has the land and the labor, but it is missing the financial resources to develop its agriculture. Situations like this can have several outcomes. In the best-case scenario, both parties have the best of both worlds and they will mutually benefit from the cooperation. In the worst-case scenario, they will both have the worst of both worlds and tragedies will happen. The future events and results will depend on the quality of the respective leaderships and on their aptitude to manage human nature for the best, or not. China is investing large sums of money in Africa, and not only for agricultural development. They also help many local small businesses to develop and grow. This is a smart approach, because economic development will benefit the host countries in the long run. China has experienced the result of its own transformation from a poor rural country on the verge of famine for decades into a modern industrialized country with a growing middle class. That part of their experience is quite valuable for African nations. Hopefully, China will also learn from the heavy environmental cost that it is paying and is going to pay for a long time to come. If their leaders can learn from the past, there are reasonable chances of success in these ventures. If they do not learn from their mistakes, then the host countries will reap the bad seeds that they will have sowed. Opposite to this long-term and comprehensive approach of economic development beyond just agricultural development is the case of land purchases by the late Libyan leader Gaddafi. Libya bought land in Western Africa in 2011 and it told the local farmers that by the end of 2011, they would have to leave. These farmers had worked the land for years and have probably no other way to make a living. What will happen to them seems to interest nobody. Ethiopia is also in the process of selling a lot of land to foreigners, and they expel the local farmers. The government does not offer them any retraining or any other possibility to start a new life. The farmers are left to their own devices. If Ethiopia ever harvests a storm, they will have to remember when they sowed the wind. The path towards a plentiful agricultural production in Africa will be long. It will not be easy. It will take time to build a proper infrastructure, to access the money necessary to modernize the continent, to fight corruption, to eliminate poverty, to improve health and to solve the problem of unclear land proprietary rights. However, the potential of the land is there, regardless of who owns it, and who the leaders are and will be. Africans will figure out how to solve the proprietary rights in the future. The execution, on the other hand, depends entirely on who leads the actions and how the society functions. The human factor will decide of the success or the failure.

Yield improvement can take place everywhere. Even the USA has room to improve further. During National Agriculture Week 2011, one piece of the news was that in 2010, one US farmer provided on average for the needs of 155 people, while in 1960 this number was only 26. This statistic is interesting because it can be deceiving, actually. Is this number as good as it sounds? Of course, for many in the US agriculture, this number of 155 is the best proof that US farmers are the best in the world, and that large-scale industrial agriculture with help of massive technology and mechanization is the best there is. The statistic needs further analysis. It is only during 2011 that China became the first export destination of US agricultural goods, finally passing Canada and its modest population of 34 million people. That does not sound like much volume. What the National Agriculture Week news did not mention was the total number of farms in the USA.

The number of farms dropped from four million in 1960 to 2.2 million in 2010, according to the data from the US Census Bureau. Going from 26 to 155 would have been very impressive if the number of farmers had been stable, but this is not the case. Some simple math shows the true evolution. In 1960, four million farmers fed 26 people each. For the whole country, this meant that the US agriculture fed four million times 26, or 104 million people. In 2010, and by keeping the number of 2.2 million farms, the same calculation, 2.2 farmers times 155 people fed per farmer, comes down to 341 million people fed by US agriculture production. Instead of increasing six-fold (155/26) as the news tended to imply, the actual increase is of only 3.3 times (341/104).

Over a period of 50 years, this represents a year-on-year increase of people fed by US agriculture of only 2.4% on average. It is higher than the average year-on-year increase of the world's population over the same period, but it is far from exceptional. As an indication for comparison, the world's food production has increased on average by 3% year-on-year over the same period, according to the FAO. The math shows us that the number of people fed by one farmer is not a good indicator of the actual performance of the national agriculture. In the case of the US, the number of 155 only indicates that there are fewer farmers, that they have to manage large farms, and that machines and equipment have replaced human labor. The number of people fed per farmer is not an indicator of yields. Being bigger, more intensive or having more technology does not necessarily mean being more efficient. It has to be the right size, the optimal level of intensification and the proper use of the right type of technology. A much more relevant number is the number of people that one hectare of land can feed. Yield is the true key indicator for efficient agriculture.

It is interesting to compare different parts of the world. India is often presented, especially in the Anglo-Saxon press, as a country that does not address agriculture challenges properly. According to these reporters, India should be a lot more like the US, going big and industrial, instead of keeping its large rural population. Indian agriculture certainly needs some reforms, but the many differences in terms of demographics and socio-economic situation also influence policies. India has 1.2 billion inhabitants, and statistics indicate that 200 million people are malnourished. This implies that one billion people are fed "reasonably". In India, close to 70% of the population is in rural areas, while in the USA, the agricultural population is less than 1%. The population density of India is 10 times higher than the American population density. If the USA had the same population density as India, there would be three billion Americans. How would Americans think in terms of food security with such a population? Could they feed reasonably one billion people?

The statistic of National Agriculture Week tells that currently only 341 million of them would have food from their domestic production. In such conditions, it is very likely that meat consumption would be much lower in the USA than it currently is. The rate of obesity would probably be much lower, and producing biofuels would meet much more resistance. American agricultural policies would be quite different. Compared to India, the USA is an empty country. However, this comparison may not be the best to make. After all, the Indian diet is rather different from the American one, and India still needs imports to feed its people. A region that is closer to America in terms of eating habits is the EU.

Hardly a week passes by without some article from US industrial agriculture media that criticizes Europeans to resist the American model, especially GMO crops. According to the biased pundits, Europe is losing ground because of this shortsighted stubbornness. There again, some math can help. Once again, the population density will provide us with insight. If the USA had the population density of the EU, there would be 1.1 billion Americans. Once again, that is much higher than the 341 million that American farmers can feed. As far as the EU is concerned, the region is food secure, and in most European countries, the yearly per capita consumption of meat is close to 100 kg. There is no food scarcity problem in the EU.

In this case, we are not comparing meat eaters and vegetarians. Just as it looked that India was doing not such a bad job at feeding its people, considering the circumstances, the EU actually delivers an enviable performance.

What the math really shows is that the world is very diverse. It is diverse from demographic, economic, socio-cultural, climatic, agricultural points of view. Mechanical thinking is convenient but not effective. Agricultural policies must consider all the social and environmental variables and must be adapted to the specific environment to meet food demand optimally. There is no universal model, and there does not need to be any.

The focus must be on producing the highest yields possible in a sustainable manner in the most optimal manner in the specific local conditions. Thus, farmers can repeat and improve on solid performance for generations to come. To grow food, the world needs good seeds, adequate amounts of water, fertile soil, proper financial resources and skilled farmers who manage resources efficiently.

Since there are so many factors that can influence food supply, it is legitimate to wonder whether it is possible to feed the growing population. The numbers presented above show that in terms of nutritional needs, the answer is yes. It shows that the limiting factor is more the infrastructure and the human factor than agricultural production. Another interesting approach is the one developed by Professor Dr. Martin K. van Ittersum, of the University of Wageningen. He determined the amount of biomass needed by a world population of nine billion people in 2050, according to different scenarios of consumption and use of agricultural products. He expressed the current need in biomass to seven billion grain equivalents (GE) for 2011. For his work, he identified three scenarios. The first scenario is in the case that agriculture produces only for feed and food. The biomass requirement would be of 12 billion GE. The second scenario includes the demand of the first one, plus a production of 10% of energy supply coming from biofuels. The biomass requirement is then of 17 billion GE.

The third and last scenario is the one of a world population living on a Western diet. The demand for biomass is of 23 billion GE. This number is more than three times the current one. Dr. van Ittersum compared this with the production potential. In the best case scenario, which would eliminate waste and having crops producing at their full genetic potential by being able to utilize all inputs optimally, the production could reach 32 billion GE. If agriculture could use only half the water it requires for its irrigation needs, the biomass production could reach 27 billion GE.

The conclusion of his work is that the Earth has the potential to feed and cover the needs of the 2050 population. The challenges are many to increase production and increase the yields, but it is possible, with a reasonable buffer. However, many actions are necessary, and so is good leadership, if the world wants to succeed. His study also includes the diet and the use of agricultural products in a rather "luxurious" situation. One can wonder whether the Western diet, with all its excesses in consumption is desirable or reasonable.

How Diet Makes a Difference

As the economy in emerging countries is improving, their population becomes wealthier. Just as it happened in Western countries during the 20th century, the increase in wealth translates into dietary changes. The consumption of animal protein, especially the consumption of meat, increases.

To realize what the consequences of a higher consumption of meat might be, it is interesting to make calculations for China. When 1.5 billion people eat on average one more kg of chicken meat per person, world production needs to increase by about 750 million chickens. That represents about 2% of the world's production. Similarly, when each Chinese consumes on average one more kg of pork, the world must produce 15 million more pigs. That number represents 1.5% of the world pig production. For beef, an increase of consumption of one kg per capita per year means the need for a production of 2.4% higher than today.

Meat consumption in China has already passed the milestone of 50 kg per capita per year, and projections indicate that it should reach 80 kg per capita per year in 2030. Clearly, consumption will increase by much more than just one kg.

An increase of 10 kg of chicken meat per capita per year in China means that the world's chicken production would have to increase by 20% to meet the new demand! This represents almost the entire US chicken production volume, and more than Brazilian production. In the case of pork, an increase of consumption of 10 kg per capita means that the world's pig production would have to increase by 15%. That is five times the current pig production of Iowa, USA. That is 60% of the EU production.

For beef, the world's production would have to increase by 24% to meet an increase of 10 kg per capita per year! This number also represents about 125% of the current total US beef production.

Different animal productions have different feed conversion ratios (FCR). The FCR is the quantity of feed needed to produce 1 kg of meat. For chicken meat, the FCR is of 1.8. For pig meat, the FCR is about 3. For beef, depending on the proportion of grass in the cattle's diet, the amount of grain used to produce 1 kg of beef varies. With an average FCR of 3 for the various types of meat productions, an increase of meat consumption of 30 kg in China would result in the need to produce three times 30 kg times 1.5 billion. Depending on the consumption of which type of meat will grow the fastest, the need for feed, excluding grass, would vary between 100 and 150 million tons.

The world's second largest population, the Indian population, is still largely vegetarian. Although India is among the countries with the lowest meat consumption, with less than 4 kg per capita per year, Indians are gradually changing their eating habits. Meat consumption is increasing in India, too, but not in proportions as dramatic as in China. Nonetheless, with a growing population, any incremental meat consumption will have physical consequences. Some simple math can show the magnitude of the higher demand for meat.

Between 2010 and 2050, the world's population will increase by 2.2 billion, from 6.8 billion to nine billion. If everything stays equal, the consumption would increase by about a third (2.2/6.8). According to the FAO, the average consumption of meat per capita in the world in 2010 was of about 47 kg. The population growth alone would represent a meat consumption increase of 2.2 billion times 47, or 103 million tons. This number represents about a third of the 2010 meat consumption.

In the example of China mentioned earlier, the predicted increase of 30 kg per person represented an increase in meat consumption of 45 million tons.

Even if the world average meat consumption per capita remained stable between 2010 and 2050, the need for additional meat production would be of 2.3 (103/45) times the numbers in the China example. This represents an additional need for animal feed, excluding grass, of between 230 and 345 million tons compared with 2010.

The situation becomes even more interesting when the average consumption per capita increases. For every 10 kg increase of individual consumption, the need for additional meat production increases by nine billion times 10 kg, or 90 million tons of meat. For each 10 kg increase of average meat consumption, an additional volume of 600 to 900 million tons of animal feed is necessary. The following table presents the effect of the population increase to nine billion people and its meat consumption on production volumes.

Average individual meat consumption increase from 2010 (kg/capita/year)	0	10	20	30	40	50
Average individual meat consumption (kg/capita/year)	47	57	67	77	87	97
Total meat consumption (million tons)	423	513	603	693	783	873
Total meat consumption increase from 2010 (million tons)	103	193	283	373	463	553
Percentage of increase from 2010	32%	61%	89%	117%	145%	173%

An average meat consumption of 97 kg per capita per year would be about the current average of developed countries. If the average meat consumption per capita per year in the world were to meet such a number, meat production would have to almost triple from 2010 volumes.

Most of the gloomy scenarios about the challenge of feeding the world are based on the assumption that the diet model would have to be the Western diet, and in particular the American diet. This is far from certain. Actually, it probably will not be the case. As the world's population increases, one of the sensitive issues, especially in the overfed world, will be what to eat and how much of it. Higher food prices will also force people to indulge less. It is important to understand the difference between nutritional needs and consumer desires. Today, the world produces enough calories and protein to meet the actual nutritional needs of nine billion people. If the nine billion people expected for 2050 all want to have a Western diet, the amount of calories needed would be equivalent to the nutritional calorie needs of 17.5 billion people.

It would be normal to expect feed conversion efficiency to improve in the future. Nonetheless, the production for animal feed would then increase with 3,000 to 4,500 million tons above the volumes necessary in 2010. Since a third of grain production goes to animal feed, a tripling of meat production means that grain production would have to double, just because of the desire for more meat.

Clearly, the challenge of feeding the world will depend increasingly on meeting the demand for meat. The challenge for producers of agricultural commodities will be to keep up with the demand for animal feed. As demand for meat increases, there is no doubt that more and more questions will arise about how much meat the world can afford to eat. The world food situation will depend on how much meat people want to eat, not on calorie count.

How much meat should we eat? The vegetarians have a simple answer: none. Intuitively, everyone can understand that competing for grains with animals means less food is available for people. It is worth calculating an estimate of how much food universal vegetarianism would free, and how many more people could be fed.

Meat contains approximately 75% of water. The rest consists mostly of protein, fat and some minerals. Fat contains 9 calories per gram and protein contains 4 calories per gram. The fattiness of meat varies between species and cuts.

To give a slight advantage in favor of the carnivores, the calculation will use an average of 6 calories per gram of the mix protein-fat, which represents only 25% of the weight of meat (100% minus 75%). With this assumption, one kg of meat would contain 250 grams times 6 calories per gram, which equals to 1,500 calories per kg of meat. On average, it takes 3 kg of grains to produce 1 kg of meat, and grains contain about 15% of water. The rest is a combination of carbohydrates, protein and fat. The proportions of these three components vary, depending on the type of grain used. Wheat or corn will contain mostly carbohydrates, and some protein. Soybean contains a high level of fat. Carbohydrates contain 4 calories per gram. The calculation will use an average of 4.5 calories per gram of the mix of carbohydrates, protein and fat. Three kg of grains, at 4.5 calorie per gram minus 15% humidity contain 11,475 calories (3,000 x 4.5 x 85%).

Since the average meat consumption is 47 kg per capita per year, the average human being consumes 70,500 calories per year (47 times 1,500) from meat. The number of calories from the equivalent of grains is of 47 x 11,475 = 539,325 calories per year. The meat eater would need to keep consuming his 70,500 calories. The excess calories would then amount to 539,325 minus 70,500. This equals 468,825 calories per year, or 1,284 calories per day. This amount represents about two thirds of the number of calories a human being needs on a yearly basis. If each average meat eater switching to vegetarianism would free food for an additional half person, 7 billion people switching to a vegetarian diet would free enough food to feed 4.5 billion people. As mentioned, the calculation used gave a conservative advantage in favor of meat. The number of calories per kg of meat is on the high side. With the same bias, the average amount of calories in the grain diet was set conservatively low on purpose. Even with a waste of food of 30%, as is the case today, a universal vegetarian diet could feed 11.5 billion people in 2010. To be fair, the diet would not have to be vegetarian because the calculation did not include the use of grass by ruminants.

Ruminants are the only way to transform grass into food, and they are quite useful in this regard. They produce milk and meat from grass. This is even more important to mention, as the world area of grassland is twice as vast as the area of arable land, where the grains must be produced.

What the calculation does show very clearly is that humanity's future diet will directly influence global food security and stability. The world will live with the consequences of the actions of its people. However, the good news is that should things go dire when trying to meet the demand for animal protein, all that would need to happen to bring things back in balance would be a drop in meat consumption. Adjusting the diet to the production ability of agriculture could work like a safety valve.

Is the conclusion of this calculation that we should all become vegetarians? It is not. Meat has a special place in human food psychology. Vegetarians should recognize this fact, too. The fact that so many vegetarian products mimic meat almost to perfection shows that the look and the texture of meat appeals to a broader audience than the sole carnivores. Meat is tasty and enjoyable. As long as meat consumption does not cause food supplies or the environment to be in trouble, there is nothing wrong with it. Is there an optimal amount of meat that can prevent agriculture to overheat, and yet be satisfying at the same time? After all, a significant amount of meat is consumed in such a way that it would not make much of a difference it was replaced by a vegetal alternative. The true meat connoisseur cannot taste much of his/her favorite ingredient in many preparations. Deep-fried sandwiches and other nuggets taste all the same, regardless of which meat is inside. It would taste just about the same if it was a textured soy alternative.

Proteins come from diverse sources in our diet. To calculate how much meat is optimal from a nutritional point of view, it is useful to make some assumptions. A diet of 2,500 calories per day is sufficient for most men with normal physical activity.

The share of carbohydrates to provide calories is of about 60% to 65%. This represents a range of 1,500 to 1,600 calories per day. Within the carbohydrates group, sugars should not exceed 40%. The rest should come from starch. As carbohydrates contain 4 calories per gram, the quantity of starch needed is 1,500-1,600 times 60% divided by 4, which is about 180 gram per day. Starch can be found in many foods, such as bread, rice, pasta and potatoes.

Next to starch, these foods also contain protein in various proportions. On average, a content of 10% protein is a good approximation. Since the ration needs to contain 180 grams of starch, the quantity of protein that these foods bring in the diet is of the order of 180 grams divided by 90%, which equals 20 grams per day.

A balanced diet contains a variety of foods. A quantity of milk and dairy equivalent to 250 ml of whole milk is reasonable. There is about 4% protein in milk. This brings the amount of dairy protein to 10 grams per day. A consumption of five eggs per week will bring 5 times 6 grams of protein per egg over 7 days. Per day, this is an average consumption of 5 grams of protein per day. Fish a good source of protein, and it should be eaten at least twice a week. For a consumption of 125 grams (4.5 oz) per week in two meals, fish brings a quantity of 50 grams of protein. Calculated on a daily average, fish provides 7 grams of protein. A balanced diet should also contain beans. A consumption of 125 grams of beans per week would provide 50 grams of protein, or on an average daily basis 15 grams.

Nutritional recommendations for daily need of protein vary depending on the sources. The most common number is 0.7 gram of protein per kg of body weight. A man of 70 kg would need 50 grams per day, which is also the recommendation of the US government. The needs of men are higher than the needs of women and children.

Adding up the previous numbers gives the following table:

Food type	Average g of protein/day
Bread, rice, pasta or potatoes	20
Dairy	10
Eggs	5
Fish	7
Beans	7
Sub-total	**49**

Of course, the previous table shows an example of a diversified diet. It is everyone's choice to eat as he or she pleases. However, the table shows that a balanced and diversified diet that meets the needs for protein does not require a lot of meat.

Eating large quantities of meat is a personal choice. The Western diet, at about 100 kg of meat per capita per year, provides a lot of protein. At 20% protein in meat, 100 kg per year represents an average daily supply of about 55 grams of protein. This is more than a person needs. The American diet, at the time of its peak of 124 kg per capita per year, supplied a daily average of almost 70 grams per capita. From the above, everyone can see what is reasonable, what is a luxury and what is excessive. Consuming more meat than nutritionally necessary also raises other questions. As mentioned before, meat consumption will affect the need for agricultural production, but there is more than just the issue of producing enough food. Producing more meat means producing more manure and emitting more greenhouse gases, methane in particular. This causes several challenges and choices.

Either producers must find a way of producing more meat without increasing the quantity of manure and gases, or they need to find a way of using and treating them in such a way that they do not accumulate and cause harm to the environment.

Considering the problems of obesity and diabetes, a similar discussion is necessary for sugars. As mentioned previously, sugars should not exceed 40% of the total carbohydrates, which in turn should represent about 60% of the total calorie intake. For a 2,500 calorie per day diet, sugars should not provide more than 2,500 times 60% times 40%, which equals 600 calories per day. Since sugars contain 4 calories per gram, the daily amount of sugar should be lower than 150 grams. This number is the maximum amount, but it does not need to be matched, either.

A good source of sugars to meet the body's need is fruit and vegetables. Depending on how much of these a person eats, he/she will be able to cover more or less of his/her needs. Within the maximum limit for sugar intake, consumption of added sugar is fine, although optional. Sugars have received bad publicity. So have fat and meat. Industry lobbies fight back by trying to prove that their products are not responsible for the rising health issues of obesity, diabetes and heart disease.

Are carbohydrates, fats and meat bad for consumers? The answer is that the question is not addressing the right issue. Carbohydrates, fats or meat are harmless as long as they are consumed with moderation and within the limits of nutritional needs. In the process of evolution, Nature arranged metabolism in such a way that humans, as well as other species, could survive periods of food deprivation. On good days when food would be plentiful, people would eat more than they need, but the excess calories would not be lost. They are stored in the body in the form of fat. Body fat creates a reserve that would prove useful for the days when the hunters and gatherers came back to the cave empty-handed.

In a situation when food is largely available everyday and quite affordable, as it is the case in more and more countries, people actually would not need to have this metabolic buffer anymore for excess calories. Since they eat several times a day, every day of their lives, the calorie buffer mechanism has become superfluous. Unfortunately, evolution has not kept up with the pace human societies have organized to provide food all the time. The result is that all excess calories are still metabolized into fat. In the case of the USA, where people consume 3,800 calories a day on average, they consume much more than they need. The FAO estimates on average the daily calorie need of a person at 1,800. The excess calories become body fat. When people consume so many calories every day, they store fat every day, too. Since the number of 3,800 is the country's average, a number of Americans consume more than twice the number of calories they need. In such a situation, obesity should not come as a surprise. When it comes to nutrition and food, carbohydrates and fats are not bad. They are indispensable nutrients that help the functioning of the body by providing the nutritional elements necessary to live healthy. When consumed with moderation, carbohydrates are good, fats are good, and meat is good. Too much protein can cause problems, too. The nuance about eating habits is simply that consuming too many carbohydrates, too much fat and too much protein every day is not healthy. It is really a matter of quantity and of quality. It is about life choices that everyone can make. Eating right is not difficult. Yet, very few people have a diet based on their true nutritional needs. A frequent argument to blame the current food offering for diet-related ailments is that a good diet is more expensive than junk food. A simple comparison of prices[6] between widely available alternatives shows a different result. The consumer price per pound for candy bars is about $6.00 per pound, while for apples, it is $0.49 and for bananas, it is $0.59. The number of calories contained in a candy bar is about the same as in an apple or in a banana.

---

[6] I personally carried out this quick price survey in Vancouver, British Columbia, Canada during the fall of 2011. The prices may vary, but price difference between the wholesome foods and the junk food is obvious and substantial.

Similarly, the price per pound for potato chips is of $5.00, while for potatoes it is $0.39, of broccoli is $0.99, of carrots is $0.59, of onions is $0.39 and of beans is $1.00. The healthier snack is actually the gentler one on the wallet.

There is no excuse to justify giving the preference to junk food over wholesome food. People make choices, and they have to accept the consequences of their choices. Food is one of the most enjoyable things in life, as long as it is consumed with moderation. An incidental excess occasionally is fine, too. It is a sign that people enjoy life. A healthy lifestyle is paramount. A person should have 7 hours of physical activity per week. It is best not to gain extra pounds in the first place, because fat tissue is remarkably persistent.

During 2011, the organization Slow Food USA came with what they called the five-dollar challenge. The purpose was to challenge people to make meals that would not cost more than five dollars each, which is about the price of a fast-food restaurant menu. The five-dollar challenge is not much of a challenge, really. All it takes is to shop smart and to cook. Shopping smart is easy, with all the products on sale in the stores. Cooking is easy, too. In 30 to 45 minutes, it is possible to make a nice balanced three-course menu that includes a soup or a salad, a main course and a dessert, for three dollars or less.

This amount of time is nothing, especially when compared with the amount of time that people waste checking cell phones and emails for messages just to find out that they have no new messages, or with the time wasted watching TV ads for junk food. The real problem is that many people do not cook or do not want to cook.

Awareness of health consequences due to overconsumption of food is growing. Blaming someone else for obesity, diabetes and other heart conditions is pointless. Whose fault is it? Is it meat? Is it corn syrup? Is it fat? Is it salt? Is it fast food? Is it the food industry? Is it lifestyle? Is it the parents' fault? Is it the consumer? Should schools be blamed for offering snacks and soft drinks to children with the vending machines they have to finance part of their operations? Such statements appear in the news regularly.

The reality is that nobody is responsible for the whole problem, but everyone is responsible for a part of it, those who supply and those who consume. The problem will not be solved as long as people do not accept their actual share of responsibility. Eating and drinking too much, in particular too much of the wrong things, is unhealthy. There is a reason why gluttony is one of the seven deadly sins. In Western countries, people eat too much, and that should not be a surprise to anyone.

After all, nobody really feels happy with being fat or unhealthy. There is a choice to make: fit or fat? For most people, it is an easy choice. They would prefer to be fit. However, eating habits are developed unconsciously from early childhood, and switching to conscious choices is not easy to achieve. It requires willpower and self-discipline.

The seriousness of food-related health problems has already generated action. There are government campaigns. Food producers are reviewing their formulas and are working toward healthier products, in particular by lowering the content of salt and sugar of their foods. However, this is a slow process. It could take the industry another 10 years. One may wonder why it takes this long to remove a few grams of salt and sugar. According to a USDA representative commenting the new school lunch guidelines in the USA presented in January 2012, "*This will require innovation on the part of product manufacturers in the form of new technology and/or food products.*" Anyone who cooks knows how easy it is to drop less salt and sugar in food. Maybe, they should remove all the salt and sugars from consumer foods and let the consumers decide how much they want to put in their food. Everybody has sugar and salt at home. The problem with convenience is that the consumer gives up control to the producer of the ingredients used to prepare food.

More and more consumers are also adjusting their eating habits, mostly by changing what they buy and where they buy it. This attitude will speed up the evolution. This food trend is not just in Western countries.

In China, too, the demand for natural and organic foods is increasing. In India, concerns about the level of pesticides residues in food are making the headlines of mainstream media more and more often. India also has a strong organic movement. In these countries, environmental damage has reached such proportions that the population cannot ignore it. As the population becomes wealthier, it becomes more powerful in its relation to the people in power.

Obesity and diabetes have become societal issues in the USA, but other countries are following the same path. Europe and China have a rising percentage of obese people, especially young people. Even in Africa, there seems to be an increase of the number of overweight people. It is not possible to address obesity and diabetes without discussing corn. In particular, the surge in diabetes is often blamed on the consumption of high fructose corn syrup. Another criticism of corn is its use to produce ethanol to add to gasoline. A common criticism of current foods is the ubiquity of corn, in foods, drinks, animal feed and biofuels. The meat industry blames the ethanol industry for the price increase of corn and of animal feed, which squeezes the margins of the meat processing companies. The ethanol industry denies it all, and blames the food industry for not passing price decreases to consumers. Some numbers are useful to look at the situation with less partisanship.

In 2011, the USA used more than 40% of its corn to produce ethanol. This is more than the volumes used to feed farm animals. Since the USA produces about half the corn in the world, about 20% of all the corn grown on Earth goes to the production of ethanol. Activists groups denounce the production of ethanol as a cause of hunger in the world, as using corn for fuel takes away food from the hungry. In 2011, the area of corn in the USA was of 88 million acres. Thus, the area of corn for ethanol was of more than 35 million acres. How large is this area really? This is the size of the state of New York. It is twice the size of Ireland. It is slightly smaller than Tunisia or Bangladesh. It is half the size of New Zealand.

The expressed reason of the US government to produce ethanol is to reduce the dependence of the USA on foreign oil, especially from hostile countries. However, the main oil supplier to the USA is Canada, a friendly country. Moreover, ethanol is included in gasoline to a level of 15%. If Americans had driven cars that had the same gas mileage as the Europeans, the consumption of gasoline would have been lower by more than a third at least, which is already more than twice the level of inclusion of ethanol.

American ethanol producers are exporting, to Brazil among others, where ethanol production costs with sugar cane are lower. Clearly, they already produce more than the needs of the USA. Ethanol production and exports are subsidized. This raises the moral question of feeding the world versus feeding cars with the help of taxpayers' money, while the same taxpayers will end up paying more for meat in part because of the ethanol subsidies. If diverting food for domestic energy strategy is already controversial, diverting more food than necessary is even more controversial. Clearly, human actions look different when looked at from different angles.

Concerns about the environment grew in Western countries during the 1960s and 1970s, just a couple of decades after the beginning of the consumption society became the dominant model. It will take less than a couple of decades for a similar movement to gain full momentum in emerging countries. History repeats itself. Emerging countries will no longer accept to be the landfills of the West. Their populations will no longer accept living according to standards that are inferior to those in Western countries. If they are as wealthy as the Westerners, or even more so, as it is likely to be in the future, why should they accept living in a contaminated environment? They should not. The Westerners would not accept it. Everywhere in the world, the trend towards healthier and more natural food is growing and it will not stop.

If some people are taking action to improve their diets and their impact on the environment, this voluntary choice is still a minority of the population, today. One of the reasons for this is that healthy diets seem more expensive than the junk food.

As mentioned earlier, those who can cook know that it is quite simple to make delicious balanced meals for less than the price of the unbalanced supersized combo deep-fried so-called menu.

Internet access has made it easier than ever before for almost anyone around the world to access information, and unfortunately misinformation and disinformation as well. Secrets can no longer be held secret. Future replicas of Wikileaks will pave the way for whistleblowers to post information about questionable practices. The digital global village is likely to function in the same way as real villages do. Social control and gossips will regulate what happens globally. Transparency will be the best policy. Everyone will know everyone's secrets. The food industry must prepare for a consumer with a new take on food, instead of trying to resist change. Those who will meet consumers' expectations about products and processes will outperform their competitors. The others will disappear eventually. There always is resistance to change, and changing eating habits voluntarily may be even among the most difficult challenges. Changing eating habits in the future will not be only about voluntary choice. Food prices will also make people change the way they eat.

We Will Reap What We Sow

Money Matters

Because of the economic crisis of 2008, the global economic situation will remain fragile for many years. One of the symptoms is the nervousness about currencies. All it takes is a rumor to see a particular currency drop within minutes. The actions taken by central banks during the financial crisis have consequences. The amount of debt and the ability, or inability, of individual countries to manage the situation will influence the relative strengths of all currencies.

One currency has a special status. The US dollar is the currency for commodities. This special status also influences the actions of financial markets. Since the stock market plunge of October 2008, investors have become cautious. The value of stocks and commodities does not seem to follow fundamentals anymore. A lot of cash has left the markets and, more than before, the active players in the market place their bets for short-term returns. Most transactions are computer-generated. Software programmers have developed algorithms that allow computers to make transactions based on technical analysis within a millisecond. This may be a technological beauty, but such programs act mechanically, in a very sophisticated manner of course, but mechanically nonetheless. When it would have taken half an hour for traders to panic, the computer can now deliver the same result in less time than it takes to blink. Moreover, investors, and especially speculators, borrow large sums of money to play with derivatives instead of doing so with the actual assets. During the days when prices of commodities showed strong increases, trading volumes were quite high. On some days, in the case of oil, daily trading volumes have been as high as 10 times the actual daily consumption volumes.

For each trade, traders want to make a profit. If that happens 10 times during a day, it is not surprising that prices go up sharply. The consequences for the real economy may be rather serious. It would be interesting to see what the prices of commodities were if they were set only by the supply and demand situation of the actual physical volumes. Although there is no real possibility of knowing with certainty, some estimate that prices could be 10% to 15% lower without the derivatives.

Considering the amount of debt that the US Federal Reserve Bank has issued, also known as the amount of money they printed, the burden for both taxpayers and the American economy is heavy, and will remain that way for a long time. The bank crisis is not over. Unpaid mortgages and foreclosures will keep on weighing on the health of the financial sector and on the US housing market for quite some time.

The low interest rates may help the American economy to some extent, but the key for a true economic recovery is job creation. To consume, Americans need to make money. With the tightening of credit conditions, they now have started to save money again, instead of spending it at the mall. Before the crisis, Americans were spending on average 105% of their income, thanks to credit cards and loans based on their theoretical home equity, which supposedly would only go up. All of the above explains why the US dollar will weaken in the long-term. To alleviate this trend, the USA should increase interest rates, but as long as the economy remains vulnerable, it will not happen.

The trends for stocks and commodities prices seem to be linked to the relative strength or weakness of the US dollar. Commodities have become currencies. When the US dollar drops in value, stocks and commodities go up. When the US dollar increases, stocks and commodities go down. The logic behind this is simple. Investors are interested in protecting the value of their capital. Instead of owning actual dollars, they prefer to own assets. This is why the demand for materials, oil and agricultural commodities is firm. By switching from cash to finite resources, investors try to ensure that they will be protected from the erosion of the currency, at the very least.

Most of the demand is not for the real commodities, though, but for futures contracts. By borrowing money, they can buy even more of such investment vehicles than they normally would, or should. The higher demand for commodities results in an increasing price, in US dollars that is. Since they buy as the US dollar weakens, they will get more dollars back when they sell, although with the potential depreciation, this might not be much of a profit, but at least it is not a loss.

The demand for commodities on paper will be higher than the physical demand, and because the focus will be in the price expressed in US dollars only, food inflation will hit globally. The exchange rate between other currencies with the US dollar will not be taken into account immediately. This will happen when consumers start to offer enough resistance. The resistance can manifest in a reduced consumption of consumer goods in rich countries, but it can take the form of riots and violence in poor countries. The high price of animal feed ingredients is already a concern for companies involved in animal production. Processors will face a dilemma between a decrease of their margins and the need to run their plants at full capacity to keep costs down. Their margins and the farmers' margins will be under pressure, because the retailers will resist price increases as long as they can to keep their sales strong. Another area of margin pressure for farmers will come from the price of inputs, fertilizers in particular. If the rumor, based on paper contracts, turns into the idea that demand for agricultural production is really increasing sharply, suppliers will hike their prices as soon as they can. If farmers get higher prices for their products, they also will pay much more for their inputs.

A number of financial products and practices have led to the creation of bubbles, of which the credit crisis has been one of the worst on record. The functioning of financial markets, and in particular the markets of derivatives, has been raising many questions. In particular, the price of commodities has raised serious concerns about how the trading and market regulation – or the lack of it – have played a role in the increase of the price of food and about the possible social consequences.

Governments are trying to gain more control of markets, although they are the ones who have allowed the gradual deregulation of the financial sector, with some of the consequences that have taken place.

Derivatives create a distortion when all sorts of related products replace actual commodities, allowing more trading volume than the available physical volume of hard assets. Combining derivatives with credit further enhances the effect of the imbalance. Warren Buffett, the famous investor and one of the richest men on Earth, once described derivatives as weapons of mass destruction. They have that potential, indeed. This is why their use must be monitored closely and regulated appropriately. To achieve that, governments also need to have leverage on the financial sector. Lately, this does not seem to be the case, and most of the recent reforms that have been passed in various parliaments will be implemented very slowly, and have been weakened under pressure of the financial lobby. This does not bode well for the future. This will be another case of reaping what has been sowed. The latest harvest was in 2011.

The fingers are pointing to speculators, although without clearly defining what a speculator is. Speculation is not new. In the past, there have been many examples of speculation. The stock market collapse of 1929 also had some of its causes in speculation. There is a dose of speculation in every investment. Investors put their money at work where they expect it to grow. They never have certainty, but they hope that their preferred scenario will come out. For as much as speculators can cause damage, it is also only fair to say that they speculate on what they believe is the most likely to happen. They do not mismanage companies, they do not burden countries with debt, they do not make the weather, but they act on these factors. Often, their actions just amplify a trend and trigger the next event. On some occasions, they may create such events, but generally, they only accelerate the inevitable to happen. Activities of speculators are good indicators of where the system has weaknesses and what problems need urgent fixing. Financial markets are about one thing only: money. Speculators do not care for other people. They care only about making money for themselves.

Markets are also a reflection of how the economy, countries and the listed companies are performing. Markets do not choose a side in particular. They anticipate and react to events and trends. Markets in general are the place where supply meets demand and prices are adjusted to reflect the situation of the economy. If there is too much of something, prices drop to a point that some suppliers choose not to continue producing. Then supply adjusts to actual demand. If there is a shortage, more suppliers are attracted to participate until prices help adjust supply with demand. It is true for farmers' markets, were people might decide or not to buy their food, depending on the prices. Some people choose to, but others decline. The same statement is true for supermarkets and any other market place or store. The market is the place where money and products change hands.

This distortion of power in financial markets and the increased focus on short-term return also affects how businesses function. Investors who put their money in stocks expect the prices of their shares to increase. That is normal. Unlike several decades ago, when only wealthy capitalists invested in stocks mostly for the dividend, today's money managers want a quick and strong return. A few percent return a year does not interest them. They aim at double-digit return numbers. Some investors go even further. They buy as many shares as they can to be able to influence strategic decisions by companies. They interfere with the executive boards and the management of these companies. It is good to make sure that CEOs are focused on the right things, but the interference can become disruptive for the proper functioning of a company. It creates tension within the staff. It triggers many rumors in the markets and it sometimes causes strong fluctuations of the share price. This does not help to create value for shareholders, but it is attractive to short-term speculators.

Everyone who follows quarterly company results presentations will notice one thing. It is all about financial results. Although almost every company listed on the stock exchange has CSR (Corporate Social Responsibility) policies, as well as social and environmental sections in its annual report, questions from market analysts never address the social performance or the environmental performance.

In quarterly results presentations, future projections are usually about the following quarter, or the next couple of following quarters, but not much farther ahead than that. The pressure from financial markets on companies' management to perform always better always faster favors the short term instead of the long term. Companies have to present their results every three months to the markets, and the results had better be good. The pressure of stock markets on CEOs is high. Not only do they have to deliver good results, they must also present plans that deliver strong growth. Presenting a plan with single digit year-on-year growth will not work, even if the company would actually deliver healthy results. This pressure pushes companies to always develop more sales, more products and enter new markets. This is not all bad. Innovation is necessary to build a better future, and developing new business is a way for companies to strengthen their position, as long as the timing is right and the markets are ready. Unfortunately, this is not always the case. The pressure to deliver always more, and always faster, brings sometimes companies to stretch themselves thin or to venture in new activities when they are not quite ready. This also pushes the search for mergers and acquisitions, which if done improperly can result in serious disappointments. A common statistic is that 60% of mergers fail to deliver the expected results. Some mergers even end up in disasters.

The need to come with growth plans stimulates innovation and R&D (Research & Development). However, these activities often require substantial investments. Few new products succeed. About 60% of new consumer products are failures. R&D must be successful at bringing products that will sell for a good margin, and deliver a solid return on the investment made. If it is not, the companies will not only suffer a commercial setback, but it will post losses. CEOs do not look forward to presenting this kind of news to financial markets and analysts. It is bad for the share price. It is bad for the CEO. Acceptance by the market, and increasingly by society is not the first step.

The first step is to have new products meeting all regulatory requirements. The more regulations, the more difficult and the slower it is to pass to the marketing phase. There, too, time is money. There is an incentive to push towards less regulation, because it increases the chances of faster commercial success, and it reduces the risk of low to negative return on R&D investments.

As food is one of the very few things that people need absolutely to survive, preserving the conditions to produce food for future generations is a matter of survival of the human species, although it may not be a matter of survival for the current generation. If there were no such short-term pressure, how would farms and food companies be run? Would R&D and new product development be carried out in the same manner? Would review processes be different? Would regulations be perceived as negative? The answers are not as obvious as they seem. The pressure from financial markets is about creating value for shareholders. How can companies do this and at the same time take into account the consequences of their actions on the ability to produce enough food in the future? It is possible that financial markets should be reformed when it comes to food and agriculture. Some safeguards are necessary to preserve the long term, while ensuring that companies are managed efficiently and offer innovative products and services. There is no real-time chart for the state of the environment as there is for the share price of companies. Investors can follow the value of their stock portfolios by the second. Effect on the environment takes decades to manifest. Depending on the activity or product involved, the time that it takes for environmental effects to become visible can vary. It is very difficult to tell the number of years necessary to be sure. There is no guarantee that 10 or 15 years without apparent damage proves that there will not be any after 20 or 25 years, either.

Considering the vital importance of food and agriculture, one can also wonder whether food companies should be listed on the stock exchange at all, where all sorts of players with no connection with food production or supply can play their casino game and induce hasty decisions.

The shareholders of privately owned companies do not have the possibility to trade their shares in the way it happens on the stock market. They own the shares and they own a part of the company. It is much more than just a piece of paper. Shareholders of privately owned companies are committed and feel ownership for the long term of the company. Their reward for the good performance of the company is the dividend. There is no real-time share price adjustment. Capital gain will have to wait. Shareholders of publicly traded companies do not feel this feeling of ownership of a company and of its long-term destiny. Investors in such companies have only one goal: to sell their shares at a profit in the future. Their focus is capital gain. Dividend is just a nice bonus for the meantime. Maybe, private ownership would avoid such risks, some of them at least. Another form of ownership structure is the cooperative. It could very well be that this form of ownership will gain popularity in the future. It is also quite possible that the future format of cooperatives will include consumers among the members. The line between progress and caution is sometimes difficult to draw. It is a matter of judgment between short-term benefits and long-term risks. It is about how much control humans actually have on the consequences of their actions.

What may be the consequences for food prices? In 2008, financial markets have shown what a run on commodities can do. Unlike the 2011 strategy, the purpose in 2008 was not to protect capital. It was to force a price increase to make solid profits. Increased demand for oil futures contracts together with an increased demand for agricultural commodities futures contracts will result in food inflation. Ironically, the USA may be more vulnerable than they seem, because the price inflation will be in US dollars, and that is the only currency that they have. Food inflation would put more stress on the spending of Americans. Depending on the level of inflation, another economic slowdown is a possibility. Considering the importance of the US economy, the whole world would suffer the consequences. Reactions to food inflation will be the strongest in Asia and Africa. The situation is already sensitive, and the share of food in the household budgets is still relatively high, especially compared with Western countries.

For many people, food is already difficult to afford. The situation is such that in 2011 the Indian government offered subsidized grains to 75% of the population. This represents 800 million people. This is roughly the combined population of the EU, USA, Canada, Australia and New Zealand together. What happens with currencies, stocks and commodities exchange markets will have direct as well as indirect consequences. Everyone needs to follow the developments, because the consequences will be felt in the wallets, eventually.

Regardless of the actual causes of increasing food prices, simple economics tell that when demand increases faster than supply, prices increase. This is exactly what will happen. Even though the potential for meeting food demand, or better said the demand for nutritional needs, of nine billion people is already here, the necessary actions still need to be implemented. Important factors to succeed include reducing food waste, especially post-harvest losses, and a moderate quantity of meat in the diet. This means that people need to change their behavior towards food.

Money matters. That is a fact. This is why money is probably the best incentive for change. The future will bring plenty of incentives to change diets. The current concerns about food prices and the food riots of 2008 have created awareness about food supplies. The price hike was more the result of investors, not necessarily speculators, looking for a safe haven for their US dollars through transactions in futures contracts. However, the reality is that commodity markets, even on paper, set the official market price, which enters the real economy. This, in turn, affects the price of food for households all over the world. The poorer countries are more sensitive to food price inflation, and this has the potential to cause very serious unrest.

Since money talks, financial incentives always have effects. Subsidies are a common tool in agricultural policies. Over the past decades, agricultural subsidies have received increasingly bad publicity.

Some consider subsidies a distortion of markets that create unfair trade conditions. This is one of the reasons why eliminating subsidies is on the agenda of the never-ending WTO[7] Doha Round of negotiations.

Yet, with an increasing world population and the need for more food production, one can wonder whether agricultural subsidies really are a problem. History has shown that subsidies can be a very effective way of boosting production. For instance, subsidies have been a major element for the European Union to increase its agricultural production in the decades following WWII. The purpose of the European agricultural policy was to ensure that Europe would become self-sufficient for its food. The harsh years of food shortages during WWII had been traumatic, and the European leaders ensured that such bad times would be behind their citizens for good. Europe subsidized the production of many commodities. Subsidies work. When people are paid to do something, they usually do it quite willingly. If they are paid to not do something, they will not do it. The subsidies worked so well that Europe ended up with surpluses of butter, veal and many other commodities. Financial incentives have made European vintners pull off vines, then replant them at the same place later. Subsidies have encouraged Spanish farmers to plant many more olive trees than the olive market needed. Financial incentives to put land in fallow worked, too. Financing surpluses also cost the European Union a lot of money.

Considering how critical financing is for farmers, and that many farmers need a second job to make ends meet, some form of financial support is useful. Moreover, the world will need farmers for the future. Agriculture needs to be an attractive profession to have enough people to produce all the food needed.

---

[7] WTO: World Trade Organization

The true problem with subsidies is creating a cost-effective system. Subsidies must help produce what is needed. They must not become assistance programs, or government pensions. They are only a means. They must not become an end. Subsidies need to deliver the right incentive to be effective. They may have unexpected side effects because subsidies also modify the perception and behavior of the recipient. An example of a subsidy that seemed to aim at the right action, and yet has not delivered proper results, is the subsidy on agricultural inputs by the Indian government. They subsidize fertilizers with the idea that fertilizers become more affordable for farmers, and therefore the farmers would be able to increase their yields. As such, this is not a bad idea, but the outcome was not as expected. The result has been over-fertilization in some areas and insufficient fertilization in other regions. Fortunately, subsidies also help to create success stories. A positive example of effective money incentive linked to a comprehensive approach that involved government and private companies is the boost in rice production in Uganda. This effective policy helped increase production 2.5 times and turned Uganda from an importing country to a net exporter of rice within 4 years.

Quality must come before quantity for subsidies, too. Agricultural subsidies must be a part of a comprehensive plan towards the essential goal of feeding more people. They need to be market-driven and they should not be used to entertain a production-driven system. Some subsidies, or government support as they should be called, take many forms and many names. They include grants, market support mechanisms, export enhancement programs, specific tax regimes for farmers, and many other forms.

There is quite a bit of semantics involved. Other types of financial help that may distort the fairness of competition, although more indirect, include anti-dumping tariffs and import duties. Perhaps the stigma on subsidies comes from their being granted by governments, and government intervention is often perceived negatively. One could argue that private investments can be another type of subsidy.

After all, that money aims at encouraging more production, too. The main difference is about the kind of return. Private investors look for a capital return, while governments look for a societal return.

One of the main causes of tensions about subsidies is their effect on competition in the markets. All the players involved in world markets want the same. First, they want to have the best conditions possible to compete against others. Further, they also want to make conditions for others to compete as difficult as possible. In international negotiations, many countries would like others to cut their subsidies while keeping at least some of their own, if not all of them. Everyone always finds that only the competitors' subsidies are unfair. It is human nature.

The debate on subsidies is polarized. Too often, the issue is raised in terms of whether subsidies are good or bad. Of course, this is more a political question than one that really tries to find the truth. Subsidies are neither good nor bad. Good subsidies are good, and bad subsidies are bad. At this point, it is necessary to consider what a good subsidy should be.

A good subsidy must contribute to prosperity. It makes possible the transition from one situation to a better one. It must assist in developing production to meet demand. It should not allow the production of surpluses, which is a waste of money. It must help producers to overcome temporary start-up headwinds, as the benefits may take some time to materialize. This is why profitable activities do not need subsidies. Moreover, a good subsidy must be temporary. If an activity needs to be subsidized forever, then this activity has probably no right to exist, or something is fundamentally wrong in the way the markets function. A good policy should assess how long producers will need help and identify when they can be able to produce viably without continuous financial support.

Subsidies should be implemented only with an expiry date. It would create immediate clarity on what is expected from producers. A good subsidy is not a blank check. Producers must also commit to become profitable within a reasonable period.

A similar consideration of taxes is useful. Although it would be difficult to convince anyone that there are good taxes, it is necessary to think of which ones can be fair. Fairness is a somehow elusive concept. It is difficult to know with certainty what is fair. It is much easier to define unfair.

An interesting example is the tax on fat and sugar. Some countries, Denmark in particular, have implemented a tax on what they consider a cause of obesity and diabetes. Excesses always bring problems, and health costs are increasing. In order to finance health care, governments need money, and government revenue comes from only one source: taxes. Adding a tax on fatty and sweet foods and drinks has two effects. The first is that it makes the products a bit more expensive. The second effect is that it affects negatively the margin of the producers. An argument from the industry against the tax is that it will not deter people from eating their products, and that the tax will not work. That would be true only if the governments truly expected a drop in consumption. The first purpose of the tax is not to stop people from eating these foods and drinking these drinks. The purpose is to collect money, and hopefully to use it as a contribution to the health care system. Taxes on alcohol and on tobacco did not stop their consumption. It may have slowed it down, but people who like alcohol or tobacco keep consuming. Regardless of which health care system countries or people have, health care costs will increase, especially in aging countries. At some point, the debate will shift to responsibility and accountability. It is only a matter of time before people with healthy lifestyles will object to contributing as much for costs incurred by their neighbors' bad eating habits and poor lifestyle choices.

We Will Reap What We Sow

PART III

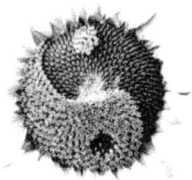

The Leadership We Need

We Will Reap What We Sow

Dealing with Issues

To succeed, the world needs leaders who can deal with issues effectively. The first step is to identify the actual problems and their causes. The main risk is to try to treat the symptoms only. It will take a discerning mind to make the distinction between symptom and cause. It may sound easy, but it is not. In this age of communication devices open to everyone, there is a lot of noise. Through all the different media, including social media, one can find many stories. The more dramatic the story, the more interest it gets. There are many myths about food security and the ability of agriculture to feed the population, now and later. Very few publications, documents and conferences present a comprehensive view of the challenges and the opportunities. Very few of them actually attempt to crunch numbers to see how they come out. In a world of short attention spans, slogans and sensation monopolize the stage.

Predicting the future is not simple. It is even more complicated when one tries to quantify the future. Numbers have a comforting character. Giving a number gives a feeling of certainty. For instance, the estimate for the 2050 world's population that is mentioned the most regularly is about nine billion people humans. Actually, the United Nations have three different scenarios for 2050. The low scenario gives an estimated population of about 7.5 billion people. The high scenario indicates the possibility of a world population of 11 billion. The number of nine billion appears only in the medium scenario. Which will be the actual number? So many factors can influence future events that there is no certain answer possible. The agricultural community needs to prepare for the most demanding scenario. It is all the world can ask at this stage.

Another example of how difficult it is to give reliable numbers is the prediction of the price of corn and soybeans made by the University of Missouri in August 2009. According to their projections, the price of corn was not supposed to exceed US$4.00 per bushel and the price of soybeans would not exceed US$10.00 per bushel through the year 2014. In June 2011, corn had already reached a price of US$7.66 and soybeans were at US$14.14. Numbers, especially about future projections are only indicative. Many factors can change the situation and deliver a different outcome.

Among those who talk about future scenarios, the doomsday thinkers are quite interesting. There is nothing like the announcement of the Apocalypse to get some attention. Statements like *"We are only one poor harvest away from a food crisis"* are just what the media needs. The reality is that the statement is true. The world is indeed only one poor harvest away from a food crisis. This is true today. This was true a in the 19th century in Ireland. This was true 3,000 years ago and it was true before that. The Apocalypse may happen someday, but until this day comes, it would be more useful to hear from leaders how humanity can avoid it. The problem with such statements is their lack of specifics. What is the definition of food crisis? The term Global Food Crisis, now known as GFC among the insiders, has made the headlines of many media outlets. Is it really possible to talk about a global food crisis when the survey mentioned previously shows that more and more people in more and more countries are overweight? Is it possible to talk about a food crisis, when the majority of people consume more calories and protein that they need from a purely nutritional point of view? It would be more accurate to talk about local food crises in a world of plenty. To be global, the food crises would have to be happening everywhere. It is not the case. The hungry people in rich countries are not food deprived because of a food crisis. They are victims of an economic crisis.

The hungry in developing countries are also victims of an economic crisis, combined with political crises. Even the billion hungry people in the world do not all have the same perspectives.

Two-thirds of the world's hungry live in seven countries: China, India, Indonesia, Pakistan, Bangladesh, Ethiopia and Congo. Economic perspectives are quite encouraging in China and India. There is a good chance that economic growth of these two countries, and the development of a stronger middle class, will help reduce the number of hungry Indians and Chinese in the coming decades. The situation in Indonesia, Pakistan and Bangladesh is still delicate, but progress is being made. Ethiopia and Congo are still facing many challenges, as is most of Africa. However, the economic situations of a number of African countries are also showing encouraging signs. Over the past four decades, the percentage of malnourished people in the world has actually dropped by half[8]. The food crises are local, not global. The world is facing many challenges, most of which can be managed and overcome. Humanity does not need slogans with little substance. It does not need apocalyptic scaremongering, either, and especially not from people with a good knowledge of food production. What humanity needs is good leadership that addresses issues with calm and determination.

Although the numbers to achieve may seem impressive, the world's agriculture has much more potential to feed a growing population than people commonly think. However, having the potential to do so does not mean that it will actually happen. Human nature has the habit of fluctuating between its best and its worst. Actions are necessary to make it happen. Success or failure to feed nine billion simply depends on everybody. Someone needs to set the course and create the conditions to take the proper actions. The world needs leaders who will make the food production potential become reality by 2050 and for every year in between and beyond.

The job description is, interestingly enough, rather reminiscent of food production and genetics. In order to express the full potential of its genes, an organism needs a favorable environment. This is exactly what current and future leaders must realize.

---

[8] See the numbers in Appendix I

They must create the conditions that will allow farmers to produce efficiently, yet sustainably. If agriculture is not sustainable, the world has a problem. Sustainability is a prerequisite.

The starting point will be about making the right decisions for both the long term as the short term. Humanity must preserve the potential to produce for future generations, but it must also provide for today as well. Proper leadership will need to take into account the interests of many different groups and manage a balanced approach between money, people and environment. For sure, future leadership will be a balancing act. This will be easier to achieve if the leaders can sell the world their plan, which means that they must have one. Leadership must have moral authority to succeed.

Leaders come from all layers of society. They come from government, industry and non-profit organizations. They can be independent farmers, or they can come from non-food related occupations. Adequate food supply is the very foundation of societies. Where there is hunger, there is no prosperity. Without food, there is no life, and just as importantly, without water there is no food. Developing food security is not an option; it is a duty. It is probably the most important policy sector of any society. This is something that nobody must take lightly, even in rich countries where people seem to take food for granted, because things may change.

What story do the leaders need to tell and execute? The points mentioned in previous chapters are a good place to start. Food waste is a scandal. It must be dealt with and it must be eliminated. In developing countries, it is caused by a lack of infrastructure. It is only a matter of money. If world leaders have the will to get that money at work, it will happen. For some reason, they are slow in doing so. Maybe it is a sign that things are not that critical for those in power.

Compared with the amounts of money thrown at financial bailouts and stimuli of all sorts since the beginning of the economic crisis of 2008, the cost of infrastructure development looks ridiculously insignificant. Such projects would actually create jobs and increase the wealth of the populations where it takes place. This would not be artificial GDP boosting, but actual poverty reduction and increased food availability. In rich countries, food waste happens at the consumer end. Food waste is one thing, but food consumption excesses or unbalanced eating habits are another area of work for our leaders. Eating more food than one needs is not detrimental for that person's health only. Food is therefore less available to others. It also forces farmers to produce more intensively. It pushes food prices up, too. What leaders need to communicate is a sense of responsibility. Wasting food is simply immoral, just like any other waste.

Food is the not the only thing that humans waste. They waste about everything they can. In the current times of worries about the consequences of the world's addiction for fossil fuels, how many vehicles are really fuel-efficient? All it takes to find out is to rent a car in North America and to rent one in Europe. The European car will have a gas mileage of at least 50% higher than its North American counterpart. In some cases, the difference will be close to twice the number of miles. Although gasoline is substantially more expensive in Europe, the cost of gasoline per mile is not very different. This fact illustrates the beauty of efficiency and it defuses the focus on price only. The input may have a higher price but the actual cost is similar. A collateral advantage is that by using less fuel, the car also releases fewer gases in the atmosphere. Financially, the operation in neutral, but environmentally the benefit is huge. Price, cost and value are very different concepts. Unfortunately, they are often considered the same. The world cannot afford this serious misunderstanding anymore.

How many machines, plants and pieces of equipment can be more fuel-efficient? Considering that the industrialized model is built on cheap energy, the answer certainly is "most of them".

The increase in the price of oil is actually a good thing. It causes inflation, which forces users to think about their fuel efficiency more seriously. Since the price of gasoline increased strongly in the USA, the most successful car classes have become middle-class cars and fuel-efficient cars. The big gas-guzzlers are out. Consumers have started focusing on the cost of gas instead of the price of gas. It has altered their criteria for choosing their cars. More expensive oil and gas will also change the economics of energy in food and agriculture. Alternative energies will become more attractive as fossil fuels become more expensive. The cost of transport and of operations will come under review and changes will be made. Higher fuel efficiency is one of the fastest ways to slow down the amount of greenhouse gases.

Water is another precious resource that has been, and still is, wasted in large amounts. The most shocking example may come from the USA. Before the economic crisis of 2008, lawns were the vegetal "production" that received the most water. It used three times as much water as all of America's cornfields did. Consumption was particularly high in the most arid regions, such as California or Arizona. In those states, water is rare and it should have been preserved. A bit of vanity, a component of pride, and some envy is just what it takes to have people do the wrong thing. A nice green patch in front of the house certainly makes someone look rich, but that water has been diverted from purposes that are more useful. The same logic applies for water as it does for energy. Water that is more expensive or simply a more limited amount available will force farmers to find new and more efficient techniques. The focus will be on making sure that the water distributed to plants is actually absorbed by the plants, instead of running off or evaporating under the hot sun.

A side effect of irrigation in arid regions is salinity. Irrigation water evaporates and leaves a white residue of minerals from fertilizers in the soil. These salts are a serious threat for yields and agricultural production in these regions. Alternative systems need to be compared by taking into account the cost of lost tonnage in the different systems.

Evaporated water is gone, purely and simply. It will not come back to the groundwater or the waterways for a very long time. Water availability is lower than before. Avoiding losses is the best way of ensuring water availability for the future. Irrigation systems and techniques will have to change. It already is happening, but much more is necessary.

Fertilizers must be used more efficiently and more effectively. In the example of nitrogen, the worldwide waste by leaching is estimated at about half the nitrogen spread on crops. This level of loss is huge and very damaging for two reasons. One reason is that the nitrogen ends up in the water system and in drinking water, making it potentially harmful, especially for pregnant women and infants. The other reason is that the production of nitrogen fertilizers uses half the world's agriculture natural gas consumption. Efficiency is not a luxury, but it is a necessity. Future fertilization techniques will have to eliminate such waste. Solutions will probably make the price of fertilizers increase, but higher efficiency will compensate. If a theoretical new nitrogen fertilizer were to be so efficient as to not suffer losses, even a doubling of the price of fertilizer per kg would allow the same cost of nitrogen fertilizer per hectare as today. There would be fewer applications required, which would reduce the consumption of fuel to operate the tractors. Production costs would remain the same at worst, but the environmental costs would decrease substantially.

The effectiveness of leaders depends on their ability to communicate and get the message across to their dependants. Changing habits and infusing a sense of solidarity and responsibility requires patience, communication and proper education programs. Defining vague objectives or using hollow populist slogans will have no effect. Only leaders with strong convictions about what ensures the future of their people, even if it means sacrifices, will be able to bring such a change. It is not easy to achieve when their countries are not on the verge of a terrible crisis. There no sense of urgency. It is easy to think that change can wait.

An interesting example about unilateral leadership is the decision of the Chinese government to slow down the number of new car registrations in 2011. They believe that there are enough cars. Getting a license plate will be difficult in the future. In 2008, they decided to ban the use of disposable plastic bags in supermarkets, thus saving an estimated 100 billion bags and the equivalent of 37 million barrels of oil per year. Similarly, China is now the world leader in renewable energies. What actions did Western democracies take on new car sales and supermarket plastic bags? When children died because of tainted milk, the Chinese authorities arrested all the people involved, and even executed two people. Of course, the use of melamine in the milk was intentional, making the case extreme. The point is not to demand imprisonment of executives as a standard operating procedure, but if executives of food companies felt that they could be held personally liable for food poisoning, the precautionary principle would apply much more systematically. It is human nature. Leaders need to demonstrate that doing something wrong comes with consequences. Although there is much to say about China's political system, one must admit that not having to think in terms of elections every four years and not having political campaigns funded by any interest group of any sort can help politicians focus in the long term, too. However, corruption and personal networks influence decisions. No country is perfect. The fact that China is plagued with so much pollution in the air, in the water and in the soils also makes the issue more acute for the leaders to resolve.

Leaders also need to be innovators. Considering how fast our world changes, and the quantity of new knowledge made available on a daily basis, many new possibilities will be available to solve old problems. Innovation is the child of human genius and, to cope with future challenges, creativity and adaptability will be major assets. It is the leaders' role to foster innovation, yet keep in mind all long-term implications.

Getting to Leadership

As the world is changing, people need to have confidence that their leaders are making the right choices. Leadership is not easy. Leaders need to be inspiring and credible enough so that other people will follow them. An effective way to evaluate the quality of the current leadership is to make a list of the leaders that would fit in these two categories: inspiring and credible. The number of politicians and heads of states that have been removed from office through elections or through social uprising indicates where political leadership stands in many countries. The growing mistrust and defiance against businesses also indicates how industry leaders are perceived. It is truly difficult to describe what makes a good leader. An alternative way to find out is to list what characteristics make poor leaders. People follow others because they believe that their lives will be better because of it. People will never accept voluntarily to have a lower standard of living, unless they realize that the temporary sacrifice will result in a better long-term situation for them than all other alternatives. Even in that case, they might be quite reluctant to follow the leader. Fear of change is not as much about change as it is about uncertainty. Fear of change is actually the fear of loss. To overcome that fear, people need to be convinced that the benefits will be more valuable than what they are about to lose.

To set the direction for a prosperous future, leaders are going to have to generate hope. They will have to be credible by proving that their vision of the future is realistic and achievable. They will have to show the willingness to sacrifice themselves if needed. People do not believe anymore in leaders that work obviously only for their own interests or those of their close friends.

People want to have political leaders who will govern, instead of campaigning for their re-election all through their mandates. People want to see companies that will care for society and environment through more than press releases, PR and vague statements. People want to see executives who will build a better world instead of focusing solely on the financial results of their companies or on their bonuses. People want to be included, not feel excluded. That is the real message behind the resentment against the 1% wealthiest. It is not against financial inequality. Unfortunately, the failure to make effective decisions about important issues such as climate, finance or food security gives a poor impression of political leaders. The average person does not feel any connection with elitist conferences such as the World Economic Forum. International conferences and world summits of all sorts seem to create a wider gap with the people. People do not really mind that those with responsibilities and high positions are rewarded well. They just do not want that to happen while they can lose everything because they do not belong to the elite circles. Moreover, they really resent the fortunate ones not showing any compassion for their misfortunes. What people want from their leaders is to show some humanity. They want to feel that, although there may be some distance, there is a connection. Arrogance, condescension and selfishness are never popular.

The future will have to be efficient. It will have to be compassionate and altruistic, too. It is not because of idealism, but because of realism. The gap between the fortunate and the less fortunate ones need to remain between fathomable boundaries. If this does not happen, then what has been going on in Arab countries since 2011 will spread elsewhere. It can happen in Europe, it can happen in China, in Russia and in the USA just as well. Most people do not ask all that much. They just want to cover their needs and feel safe. They want to be happy. This aspiration seems to have been forgotten by the leaders. It will have to be high on the priority list for the future. The objectives will have to be built around always having enough instead of having more at all costs.

Compassion and altruism can be quite effective. The future will be prosperous if the leaders work towards helping others succeed. Of all the resources on Earth, one is not depleting: the human resource. A larger population on Earth means more ideas and more brainpower. It also means more possibilities and more solutions. There is an amazing pool of talents available. Since the world's future depends on the choices and the behavior of humans, the human resource needs to be managed well. It has to be educated and trained well. Humans need to understand that they will face the consequences of their actions. Unlike the previous generations, the current one will probably face them, as time is running out to repair previous mistakes. If the stick is one option to make people do what is right, the carrot is at least as important. Nothing stimulates people more than being rewarded for doing a good job. People are at their best when they know that others appreciate what they do, and that what they do makes the world a better place. Then, they do not see their occupations as "have to" activities, but as "want to" activities.

Leaders will have to ensure that people are involved to do what they do best, that performance is not about never making mistakes, but it is about correcting them immediately. Doing so will be even more important in a world where social media of today and of tomorrow will not leave bad deeds unnoticed. Hiding and blaming will not work much longer. Transparency and responsibility will become minimum standards in tomorrow's society. Successful leadership will be about doing the right thing and doing it right. In today's debates about any industry, the word "evil" comes up regularly. Nobody would argue that there is evil in the world, but one should use the term with caution. The overwhelming majority of people go to work with the purpose of doing good work. There are many good people willing to do a good job in companies, non-profits and in government organizations. However, bad things happen indeed.

What is evil? Evil is causing harm or damage, not repairing it and not caring about it. There are two kinds of evil. It can be intentional, which is the worst kind. The evildoer knows that there will be damaging consequences to someone else, somewhere else or later.

The other kind is to let something bad happen passively. Per definition, responsibility is the ability to respond. Therefore, passivity is not a responsible behavior. It is important to underline that problems and bad things happening is not necessarily the result of evil. Everyone can make mistakes. That is human. The ancients knew this, as the Latin quote *"Errare humanum est, perseverare diabolicum est"*[9] shows. The leadership for the future will also have to look back, and learn from the past. If it fails to do so, the same mistakes will happen again, and doing the same mistake twice or more is not a mistake anymore. It is incompetence.

A good example to illustrate the need to learn from the past is the Green Revolution. After the facts, the Green Revolution of the 1960s has been criticized for having caused negative consequences on farmland. It is true that intensive agricultural practices have brought serious damage to soils and water reserves, but it is also true that the actions taken have increased food production. They averted the risk of a devastating famine in India. Today, humanity is facing the major challenge of adapting agricultural production to meet the demand of an increasing population. The term "agricultural revolution" has come back in the news and today is the time to reflect on how to handle future actions. This time, there is one major difference. With nine billion people in sight by 2050, the consequences of current and future actions will have much more impact. With the increasing population, the margin for error is about gone. Therefore, it is necessary to think ahead and consider all the things that might go wrong. It is essential to anticipate instead of waiting and having to react.

What can the world learn from the Green Revolution, then? The first lesson is that when humans decide to put all their knowledge together and give themselves the means to succeed, good things happen. Food production increased and hungry people could finally have enough to eat. The second lesson is that all actions have consequences and that it is necessary to be vigilant about what is done and how it is done.

---

[9] To err is human, to persist [in error] is of the devil

Of course, it is always easy to criticize after the facts. Pinpointing the negative effects of the Green Revolution is only relevant to a point. Using the mistakes from then as an argument not to engage in further modernization and progress is at least as destructive as bad practices implemented without thinking. Not taking action to develop new practices, new techniques and new technologies -three very different concepts- comes down to giving up. This is not acceptable. This is not possible. To meet future food demand, farmers and all the players involved in food production will need to be innovative and daring. Being innovative and daring does not mean being reckless. Recklessness is unacceptable, as the consequences could be too serious.

When looking back at the Green Revolution, the question is not so much "What did they do wrong?" as it is "Did they know something wrong would happen?" Today, it is common knowledge that heavy mechanization, intensive use of chemicals and monoculture cause soil erosion, loss of fertility and soil and water contamination. Did the farmers and the agribusiness of that time realize it was happening? Did they have the possibility to know? Some might answer "no" and others will say "yes, I told you so". Could things have been done differently, and helped feeding the people while not damaging the farmland? For the future, it is important to ask the same questions and develop a plan that helps to succeed. It will limit risks and it will offer alternatives in the case unexpected problems appear. This is quite important for Africa, where a green revolution is in the making. Are those involved going to replicate the same errors that they made in the past, or have they learned enough to avoid them? In particular, China is very active on that continent. Considering the effects of the intensification of its agriculture and water use, one can have some reasons to be a bit concerned.

To figure out what can go wrong, the best is to listen to the opponents of the practices, techniques and technologies used. In a very short time, it is possible to make a complete list of potential problems. To do this, it is also important to keep an open mind. In the past, many things that had been questioned have actually happened and caused the problems that the opponents mentioned.

It is important to realize that there are, among the critics, people with knowledge of agriculture and food. Sometimes, they have obtained degrees from the same universities as people working in the agribusiness. Contrary to the common belief, knowledge is not the privilege of one side only.

The question to answer is "What if the risks actually happen?" and to develop an extensive action plan to restore control of the situation as soon as possible at every point in the production chain and its environment. Every time progress is made, there is a struggle between the enthusiastic and those who fear change. There is a tension between action and precaution. This is quite human and normal. It is necessary to take the time to review the whole process thoroughly and accept that things do not change as fast, or not as slowly as some would like to see. In the end, progress must help humanity improve and prosper, not just in the short term. The key is to prepare for the future. The saying "*The failure of preparation is the preparation of failure*" is quite relevant when it comes to food security.

A Fresh Look at the Future

The consumption society is based on a simple philosophy. It is about buying always more. Consuming is optional, but the buying is really what matters. If consumers do not need or do not use the product, it does not matter. They simply can throw it away, as long as they do not forget to buy some replacement. To make sure that consumers buy, the goods have to be offered at low prices. To purchase their raw materials at the best prices, companies needed to have strong bargaining power, so they grew and bought other companies, and created large corporations. As labor is expensive, they looked for ways to relocate where workers would work for less money. On the other side of the negotiation table, their business partners also wanted to have stronger bargaining power, so they grew and bought other companies to create large companies, and they relocated. The result has been an increased consolidation of industries and the globalization of the economy, as it is today. The whole system has been based on cheap energy, cheap resources, cheap labor, cheap transport and easy credit, so that the consumers could spend the money they did not even earn yet.

Always more is possible only with infinite sources of raw materials and resources. Low prices are possible only with cheap resources and cheap labor. Today, things are changing. Resources are not cheap anymore, and they are going to become more expensive. Labor is going to become more expensive. Chinese workers are making more money, they have more job choice, and salaries are on the rise. All the input costs for production and manufacturing are going to increase.

Environmental issues caused by more industrial activity and more consumption are sending signals that always more is going to be very difficult. Between the 1950s and the turn of the 21st century, mass consumption was mostly happening in developed countries. As more countries develop, consumption is going to increase. The number of new consumers is staggering. The size of the middle class of emerging countries is going to be so much larger than the Western population that mass consumption Western style is unlikely to be a sustainable concept for the future.

Agriculture and food production have been through the same evolution, and the challenges ahead are not different from those of all other industrial and consumer market sectors. The *always-more-here-and-now-for-me-and-the-planet-can-wait* concept will change. The future will be about always enough today and tomorrow, instead of always more. The central focus will be about meeting the needs instead of meeting the wants. Of course, the first and most natural reaction will be for producers, suppliers, processors, retailers and consumers to resist change. That is human nature. Some of them will realize that changing the concept also offers many opportunities and they will adapt, evolve and win.

There are different ways of thinking about the future evolution of the economy. There is the linear thinking that assumes that past trends will continue. According to this approach, the system in place continues further. A common example of linear thinking in agriculture is intensification. According to a linear approach, intensifying more would deliver more volumes. Unfortunately, it does not work that way. It is only true up to the optimum point. There is a level of intensification where further intensification does not improve performance. It plateaus first. Then performance actually decreases with further intensification. Many people are confused between intensification and efficiency. They are different concepts. They go in parallel until the plateau appears. Beyond that point, they diverge. According to linear thinking, growth would be the only way forward, in continuity of the current production and supply models.

All the raw materials used by the industry eventually end up in the landfills, while the resources used deplete. In conditions where Nature reaches its sustainability limits, this approach is similar as moving forward while looking backwards. Those who resist change want to think that this approach will work.

Another approach is circular thinking, in which the economy would bring back to the environment what it takes. Old or broken products would not be thrown away. All the components are raw materials for some other production. Production processes would be organized so that the final products can be reused or recycled. Recycling would not be a voluntary choice. It would be part of the product. In such an approach, users would not necessarily have to be owners anymore. To give a familiar example, it would be similar to a library. Car cooperatives are also organized according to this concept. More business sectors will follow. For businesses, profit and share value would not be the goal, but it would be the result. As part of its 12th five-year plan 2011-2015, China has decided to include circular thinking in the development and operation of various activities.

Another way of thinking about the future would be to break the current model and imagine an entirely new one. In this approach, everything that does not work must be eliminated, and a new way of managing capital, labor and resources must replace the current model. It would be creative destruction in action.

Even when it comes to innovation, many companies still think in a linear way. The products may be different but the thinking remains. A look at the flow chart of processes shows whether this is the case or not. A growing number of companies are starting to investigate circular thinking. For instance, carmaker Renault is looking at building cars that have 95% of the raw materials coming from a recycled source and 95% of the car parts could be recycled as well. Still very few businesses use the exercise of creative destruction. When a CEO initiates an internal process to rethink completely the purpose of the company's business, challenge the future of the company's products for sustainable reasons and to reinvent the company, he/she is practicing creative destruction.

The time has come to look for new creative solutions to replace what does not work anymore or is about to reach that point. In agriculture, the objectives will be to increase the efficiency of all inputs, eliminate waste and access accurate information to make the best decisions possible when needed, more so than is already the case. Every seed will have to produce. Every drop of water will have to be absorbed by the plants, not evaporate. Every nutrient will have to fertilize plants and not the groundwater or remain on the surface of the field. Plants absorb water and nutrients through their roots. Then, why not bring them directly at the root level drop by drop instead of losing water by evaporation, creating salt crust on the surface or losing nutrients by leaching? Chemicals will have to be used when needed where needed. Every bullet will have to hit the target. Carpet-bombing of fields and of the environment with chemicals is the best way to get resistant organisms. Every action that creates a constant new environment will result in adaptation of species. This way of applying crop protection products will not be the standard practice anymore. The future economics of farming will not allow it. Every molecule will have to hit the target, not flow into the environment. Applications methods, as much as molecules, will have to be revisited.

Optimizing will also require a different design. For instance, why have manure containment exposed to precipitations? It only adds water that is expensive to transport to the fields. That is a waste of energy and time, as it takes more trips to transport diluted manure. Open manure containment also allows biogas to go into the atmosphere. It contributes to emission greenhouse gases and it is lost biogas that can be used for energy needs on the farm and for local users. When energy and water prices increase, it will sound like common sense to do so. Agricultural machines, storage systems, energy supplies, logistics, animal husbandry systems and housing, waste management, contaminant storage, etc... will all need a complete review. Even retail will deserve a fresh new look.

There are many people with many ideas. Contests may be the best way to collect these ideas and to review them. Just to name a few examples, photography, construction materials, cell phones, computers, TV sets were very different 20 years ago from what they are today. Why would agriculture equipment and methods stay the same? Today is the time to be creative. It would be useful to have systems reviewed by people with no background in food and agriculture. They would design solutions without being influenced by the baggage of linear thinking. They would focus on what the purposes of the systems are and which problems they should solve. They would not try to solve the solutions that cause problems. They would go to the essential. They might come with naïve ideas, but the "why not" angle that they would bring would be refreshing and would help rethink agricultural methods for the better. They would bring a new vision, which is exactly what agriculture needs for the future.

Creative thinking and innovation are not as difficult as they may sound. They need the right environment to flourish. A well-known example of how creative people can be is at the Australian company Atlassian. Once every quarter, the company allocates time to its employees to work on whatever they want in the way they want, and they have to present what they have created within 24 hours to the rest of the company. They have come up with more and better Ideas this way than under management supervision. People know and can do much more than they think. Humanity has so much potential to come with effective solutions for the future!

New ideas will be important in the technical area. Rethinking how to create the right incentives will be just as essential for a proper implementation. One of the most effective motivators is money. Depending on how people are remunerated, they adjust their strategy. When given a choice, people prefer to make more money than less. If the remuneration is purely financial and eliminates any incentive to think about long-term implications, people will only try to make as much as possible today, and they will not think about tomorrow. If the collaterals are included in the remuneration, then they will matter. For example, there are many subsidies in agriculture. Most of them are about producing more of something.

The subsidy motivates farmers to produce more. If farmers receive a subsidy to produce less, such as fallowing or to create wild refuges, they will do exactly that. For many years, Switzerland has subsidized farming to keep farmers in the mountains to develop and to take care of their regions. In an open and free market, Swiss farmers would probably have been out of business. Their government paid them to play a very important maintenance role that benefits the little Alpine country.

Farmers are self-employed. They make their living from their direct performance and from the remuneration system. They have to feed their families, they have to pay their bills and they have to prepare their children's future. They will choose the strategy that allows them to get the best income possible to do that. Incentives also influence the strategies of companies and of their employees. If subsidies, taxes or the functioning of markets support mostly the financial performance before social or environmental considerations, the focus will be on profit only. If there is an element of reward for socially or environmentally friendly practices that help them make more money by doing so, they will do exactly that. If farmers were to receive a financial bonus if they reach a certain yield, it is very likely that yields would increase more and faster than today. They might not succeed every year, but they would succeed more often. The carbon trade can be a source of extra income when a company emits less CO_2. Depending on how the numbers come out, reducing emissions could be a way of making more money than by keeping the emission at their current level. It does not matter where the money comes from, what matters is what is on the bank account, eventually. For executives, bonuses are an important motivator. By adapting the rules of bonuses, the focus of the management can shift substantially. For instance, if instead of profit, the bonus were based on waste reduction or on lower quantities of CO_2 per thousand of dollars of sales, the management decisions would be different. Gas emissions would be high on the priority of management teams. If the executives of seed companies were rewarded based on the yields their customers achieve in the field instead of the company's financial results only, their strategies might be different.

If sales people received a bonus only on the base of gross margin per unit and/or based on accounts receivables, instead of sales volumes, their approach to customers would be different. If bonuses in the food industry included food safety indicators, processes would change. If companies paid bonuses that include financial, social and environmental components only if the social and environmental targets were met first, regardless of whether financial targets were met, executives would certainly lead and manage differently. Of course, bonus systems have to be aligned with the overall company's fiscal environment. The decision really depends on businesses and governments. They can change the system. What really counts is that the change benefits everyone. If companies could make more money by being more environmental, why would and should they resist it? That would be silly. If executives could make more money by changing the bonus structures, why would and should they resist? This is where pragmatism is useful. There is no reason to defend a particular system. People set the rules. There is nothing wrong in setting different rules if it is the right thing and if everyone benefits. In most cases, the difficulty will lie in the transition, but that is manageable. Changing the system is a collective decision. It is necessary to change the system and harvest the rewards. This is an area where much work is needed. Regardless of how difficult it may appear at first, it will have to happen.

Leading from the Vision

To move in the right direction, the world needs leaders who can develop a comprehensive vision to build a better future. There are already many documents called visions. In most cases, they are not visions. They are brochures for strategic plans of organizations. They are more focused on what the issuer will get in the future than what the added value for the other stakeholders will be. True leaders do not work for themselves only. They have a higher purpose. They act for the collective good. By focusing on the general interest rather than their own, they meet less resistance for their vision. A new vision must include the implications and the benefits for others as well. When the proposal meets the needs of the other stakeholders, they are more inclined to pay attention and to become supporters of the project. Since they can benefit by doing so, they help promote change. Self-centered strategies are difficult to sell, because the others do not see what is in it for them. Push marketing is always more difficult than pull marketing. Push marketing is about creating wants, while pull marketing is about filling needs.

A vision that does not become action is useless. Selling the vision is an active process that takes time. Too often, impatience is an impediment to success. For the visionary, the arguments are obvious. For those who hear about it, time is necessary to understand all the ins and outs of the vision, what the long-term consequences are, and if they are willing to subscribe to the vision presented to them. There is no way to speed up the process. Communication is essential. It will be necessary to present and to repeat the ideas many times before the audience can feel comfortable with the new directions.

Selling a vision, with the objective of executing it eventually needs to follow the same steps as any other sales activity. The ideal visionary will need a number of character attributes to succeed. Next to knowledge of the topic, empathy, enthusiasm, creativity and willpower are quite useful. A strong belief in the vision together with a strong ability to convince others is prerequisite. During the sales process, qualities such as persistence and the ability to deal with setbacks will increase the chances of success. The main strength of the vision would have to include the needs of the other stakeholders. Discovering the needs and integrating them also takes time. It requires many conversations. The best way to know about the needs of another person is to ask questions. There is no point in making any assumption when it is so easy to get the answers directly from others. The original vision is not carved in stone. It will have to be amended somehow with some of the ideas and remarks that arise during the process. Listening is another essential quality in this process. People always appreciate someone who can listen to them. It makes them feel taken seriously and respected. Respect earns respect. It will serve the visionary leader beyond any expectation. It will be even more valuable as there will be some resistance along the way. Selling the vision is always a long process in which the leader needs to get the attention of others, present the arguments in favor of the vision, react as resistance and opposition appear. There is no magic trick to succeed. It is a matter of persisting. There is nothing to lose by trying repeatedly if the vision benefits society.

The most important part of the vision is the action plan. The plan is more than goals. It must include the participants and their responsibilities. It also must include timelines. This is where salesmanship will play an essential role. The challenge of feeding the world is complex and it is a massive endeavor. Nobody and no organization can do it alone. So many different areas are involved that many organizations and people will have to be involved. The role of the visionary leader will be to make sure that all those who will play a role have a sense of ownership and a sense of pride to achieve the goals. If this is not the case, then the results will suffer.

To include all the stakeholders, leadership must be collaborative. The vision and the responsibilities have to be shared. Collaborative leadership is much more than public-private partnerships. It is not just between any combination of collaborations between businesses, governments and non-profits. Sometimes, governments will have to collaborate on some projects, especially about issues that have effects beyond the limits of their borders. For instance, water management is one of such issues. As water flows between countries, water use in one country will affect its neighbors. It can possibly lead to conflicts. A good coordination of resource management can prevent such conflicts. Often, collaboration is not about one particular business sector, either. Agricultural development alone is often not enough to lift a region economically. Collaborative leadership between different industries can help develop several activities simultaneously. Synergies will appear when different economic sectors share a vision. In many cases, collaboration will have to be between the different links of an entire value chain. In the example of post-harvest losses, it is clear that all the players, from the farm to the consumer, can benefit greatly from investments. The plan to address the situation must quantify what the benefits are for every link of the value chain. For instance, if the plan shows that post-harvest losses can be reduced by 50%, what does this improvement mean in terms of respective financial benefit for the farmers, the wholesalers, the retailers, the transport companies, the storage companies, and maintenance providers? What is the share for each participant? If the plan shows an improvement of 80%, how do the numbers work? By acting in a collaborative manner with open calculations, it would be possible for the participants to estimate how much money they should invest to improve the system. The open book approach would also allow them to return the benefit in a rather fair proportion to all the investors. Although, this sounds easy on paper, the reality will be a bit more difficult. Since the approach deals with money, human nature will prevail. Unless there is an independent honest body to supervise the money flow, there is no doubt that some participants would try to get more than their fair share, and cause the project to fail.

Leadership of such projects will have to be strong, and the rules will have to be clear to everyone before the project gets started. However, doing nothing is a worse option.

When it comes to looking for partnerships as part of a value chain, one area tends to be neglected. Usually, business people will develop their business plan properly, identify their market and their source of supplies, and make sure that the math is solid. Beyond the numbers, the human factor will always play a role. Every company, every partner in the chain has its own specific culture. This is important to realize, because when cultures, and values, do not match, the relationship will always cause some hardships at some point. This is not a simple problem to solve, and usually, only few potential partners share the same values. It is also important to realize that the word "values" does not necessarily imply good ethics and honesty. Sometimes, the partner that can help grow a business the fastest might not be the right one for the long term, but it might be the best choice for now.

Depending on the region of the world, the sense of time, sometimes even of urgency, can vary a lot. For instance, North Americans tend to want to start business immediately, while the Asians will take all the time they need to find out about whom they do business with, and build enough confidence about their potential partner before starting business. In some countries, it can take several years before the first transaction takes place. A mismatch of values brings risks. It can have serious consequences, depending on how much of the business depends on the "wrong" partner. The percentage of joint ventures that fail illustrates how difficult it is. It can range from dissatisfaction about the profitability of the business, constant disagreements and tension with the business partner, to failure. One thing is sure: there will never be complete trust and loyalty when values are not aligned. This is true with collaborative projects. It is important to assess the situation before getting started.

For the future, the focus must be on helping others. By helping others to succeed, more business opportunities will be created. If the business partners share the same values and they have earned mutual respect, the result will be loyalty and long-term cooperation. Financial performance will follow, and the economic activity will grow as a result. The key question to ask will be "How can I help you?" Sustainable future growth will come only from altruism. The return on the initial investment will take time to materialize, but it will, and it will be high and rewarding for those who take the initiative. Short-term self-interest will meet resistance and long-term results will be uncertain. One of the most important ingredients for future success will be about long-term commitment and patience. Those with products and services that are actually useful to others will have no difficulty finding a buyer. Those who have the products or services that meet the needs of the market the best do not need to be pushy, impose binding contracts or act like bullies. These are the tactics of the weak, the scared and of the ones running out of time. The ones with the right products and services will need less effort to sell because the customers will simply ask for more of what is good for them. They will be loyal to their suppliers.

We Will Reap What We Sow

Helping Farmers Produce Better

Meeting food demand depends for a large part on the ability of farmers to produce adequate quantities of the food products of the right quality. To achieve such an objective, farmers depend on their business partners. To feed an increasing world population, helping farmers succeed is not an option; it is a necessity.

There is no argument against producing better. A market-driven and more efficient production reduces the amount of waste, and it increases the amount of food available for consumers. It reduces the impact on the environment and it actually reduces the cost of production. However, it is important to realize that actions to produce better are also investments, as the effect is not always immediate. From a value chain point of view, efficient production starts with high-quality ingredients. If the world wants farmers to produce higher volumes, they must have access to good genetics. Seeds that have the potential to deliver high yields, or farm animals that can produce and grow fast, while using feed and water efficiently, are an absolute necessity. Genetics and agriculture must also take genetic diversity and sustainability into account. However, with poor genetics, farmers will not be able to increase the efficiency of their production, and they might not be financially viable in the long term. Vision and proper strategy are the elements to deal with this dilemma.

Farming inputs such as fertilizers, pesticides, herbicides and animal feed, must help plants, and farm animals, to express as much of their genetic potential as possible. Suppliers can play a very important role in helping farmers use the proper products in the right amounts, in the right place, and at the right time. The same principle applies for food processors and distributors. It is their role to help farmers deliver what the market needs when it needs it.

They must encourage this by rewarding financially the farmers who do things right. This is in the interest of all the parties involved. Farmers make more money with their products. Processors get products that are more efficient to process, thus saving on costs. Distributors gain market share because they offer the right product to their customers, thus increasing customer satisfaction, appeal and loyalty. The advantage of doing things right is that it becomes more difficult for business partners to switch to a competitor. By being the best partner in business, loyalty and mutual security become at least as important as the need for complicated contractual and legal agreements.

It requires a lot of effort, commitment and communication to achieve this kind of ideal situation. Market needs must be translated to clear product specifications. To be transferred to farmers, the knowledge about how to be able to meet the required standards needs the proper channels. Access to information has become much easier with the development of communication tools such as Internet and cell phones. Smart phones and their apps are helping further, and now farmers, anywhere in the world, have much faster access to market and technical information than in the past. This helps them make better decisions faster. However, better technology and better communication tools are not enough. Extension services are crucial. Many success stories show how positive this is for food production. Telling success stories is very important. It shows what can happen when all the energies are focused on the same goal. It also creates a bit of envy, pride and greed, which is good in moderate quantities. Technical performance varies between regions, but also within a particular region, farmers have diverse technical results for a same type of production. Since yields are one of the parameters that will play a role to keep up with food demand, helping farmers improve their performance will play a central role for the future. It shows that knowledge must circulate. Only by doing so is knowledge power, indeed. When knowledge does not circulate, it may have some value to those who keep it, but it generates nothing of collective value.

Proper education and ongoing training is part of the food production of the future. In knowledge transfer, the human factor is as important as ever. Only a person who knows the farmer can know what his/her specific situation is. Knowing the farmer is the best way to help them set up plans and strategies to improve their technical and financial performance. Since farmers are independent business owners, their main concern is to generate enough revenue to stay in business, and to offer a decent standard of living and a secure future for their families. They do not farm for love only. They will choose the productions that generate the highest income for them, and they will choose their strategies accordingly. Helping them in these objectives is the way to get their attention and loyalty. Extension services need to offer the most effective solutions by taking into account the level of skills of the farmers, as well as their financial situation. Some farmers can afford and use high-tech solutions easily. Others may have money, but lack the skills to use certain techniques or technologies. Others may be technically savvy, but may lack the money. Extension service people are the ones who can help farmers make the best choices. They also must assist farmers to get the proper financing if this is the limiting factor, as long as the money would be used to deliver the proper return.

Effective extension services need strong links with research and education institutions. There must be a two-way information flow. A good understanding of what markets want is a prerequisite to pass the information to the other links in the food value chains. By starting from the market and going backward in the chain, the bottlenecks will be identified and the problems properly identified. Extension services are a good interface. They have the role and duty to define the problems to solve and to ask research to develop solutions. The issues can then be discussed within the education–research–extension triangle. Education and extension can formalize information and training formats to bring the developments from research that can be used practically on farms to eliminate the bottlenecks. Within research, it is also important to make a difference between fundamental research and applied research.

The role of fundamental research is to find out how things work. It is a purely scientific activity. The role of applied research is to investigate practical solutions, based on both knowledge from fundamental research and the practical problems communicated by extension services. When the combination of the research-education-extension triangle and the two-way information flow functions properly, farmers will be able to effectively serve markets better while performing better technically and financially. To be optimal, it is essential that this system remains independent to have access to all the knowledge and to have access to the best knowledge. In the current world, the triangle is not just local. It can and must function based on global knowledge. Here, more than anywhere else, the objective of one plus one is more than two must prevail.

In order to carry out all the necessary activities, it will be necessary to have enough people and to make sure that they have the right skills. As the population grows, food production becomes an increasingly strategic activity.

Yet, the food and agriculture sectors do not seem to have the appeal that they deserve. At the worst of the economic crisis, Californian farmers could not fill positions. American unemployed would not show interest. The farmers had to bring in people from Mexico. The work was hard on the back, but it paid decently overall, US$13.00 per hour. Attracting new people to farming and agriculture appears to be a challenging task. It is particularly clear for farming. Everywhere around the world, the average age of farmers is increasing.

It is worrying because without farmers, it will be impossible to have food. Agriculture is the foundation of society and civilization. It brings peace and security. In many countries, the jobs in food production that will arise from further agricultural development will offer many opportunities for the youth. Food production will be a pillar of the economic development of many nations.

In countries where the percentage of the active population in agriculture is low, many young people simply have never had any exposure to food production. Their food knowledge is limited to their visits to the local supermarket. Since one can love only what one knows, this seriously restricts the number of potential candidates. To get the attention of the youth, the food sector needs to become more visible and more approachable. There is a need for more interaction between education and visits to farms and food companies. Understanding food is very much about understanding Nature. Understanding Nature is about understanding humanity, and where it comes from. It is appalling to see how little knowledge city children have of food. They have lost the connection with farms and they do not know anymore what farming is about. Just like their parents, they know very little about nutrition basics. All the fad diets that emerge on a regular basis create more confusion. They need to know how to feed themselves properly. They need to know how many calories, how much protein, how much fat, and much carbohydrates they need on a daily basis. The knowledge about nutrition is essential to understand what a sound and healthy diet is. The future does not belong to a nation plagued by ailments related to food excesses. A decreasing life expectancy is not a sign of a dynamic future for a society. Understanding nutrition, eating balanced meals and enforcing food safety is the basis for proper food production. Everyone, and especially the new generations, needs to understand how critical a sustainable, safe and efficient agriculture is for humanity.

To attract new people to the food sector, it is also quite important to describe what kind of jobs the sector has to offer. The jobs need to be not only interesting, but they also must offer the candidates the prospect of competitive income, long-term opportunities, and a perceived positive social status. Many students have no idea about the amazing diversity of jobs that agriculture, including aquaculture, and food production have to offer. This is what both the sector and the schools must communicate.

Just to name a few and in no particular order, the possibilities include farming, processing, logistics, planning, sales, marketing, trade, operations, procurement, quality, customer service, IT, banking and finance, nutrition (both animal and human), agronomy, animal husbandry, genetics, microbiology, biochemistry, soil science, ecology, climatology, equipment, machinery, fertilizers, irrigation, consumer products, retail, research, education, plant protection, communication and PR, legal, management, knowledge transfer, innovation, politics and services. Working in food is much more than just being a farmer. They are many exciting and rewarding careers in the sector.

All these types of activities offer possibilities for work that can be both local and international. These jobs can be indoor or outdoor occupations. Employers are both small and large businesses. Jobs are available in industries, in government agencies, in non-profit organizations. Agriculture and food are about life sciences, and life sciences are about life. They are also about culture and quality of life. They are about the relation between humans and their environment. Not many economic sectors can offer such a broad choice of professions and experiences. Getting more students in the field of food production would require relentless communication about the present situation, as well as about future perspectives.

The first step is to re-create the connection between farming and children. It will have to start at elementary schools and continue in high school and later. Field trips should be mandatory, and lectures by people working in food and agriculture should be part of the curriculum. It is necessary for colleges and universities to envision the future. Educating students today must help make them operational for the challenges of the future. Education is nothing less than developing the human resources that will increase the prosperity, the stability and the dynamics of the societies of tomorrow. Attracting new students goes further than just agriculture and food production at large. Within food production, every sector also competes to attract new people. Some healthy competition should benefit the whole food chain.

Clearly, there is a need to identify future trends, future challenges and future needs to produce better food and more food. This will require a practical approach. Identifying future needs is not an intellectual exercise. It is about providing people with food on a daily basis for the years to come. Identifying future challenges is a team effort between education, research, farmers, businesses and governments. All must work together to create a more secure future. If we want to avoid suboptimal solutions, there cannot be gaps between the links of the food production chain.

The most effective way to work towards developing the proper curriculum and attracting students for the jobs of the future is to have a market-driven approach. The question is not only about what type of jobs will be needed, but also where they will be needed. To be effective in this process, it is necessary to develop a vision of the things to come for the coming 10 to 20 years. In this fast-changing world, today already belongs to the past. Developing a curriculum on current issues will not prepare students properly for their professional lives, and neither will it serve society properly. Only by identifying what skills will be needed is it possible to offer the best job perspectives for future food professionals, and being able to overcome future challenges.

Identifying the challenges of the future indicates where the best job opportunities are. The action plans to develop tomorrow's curricula will depend greatly on geographic location. Clearly, India, China, North America, Europe, Arab countries, Africa or Latin America will face very different demographic, environmental and economic situations. However, when it comes to food, all countries will become even more globally interdependent than they are today. This offers many opportunities to train people for work abroad, too.

From Vision to Execution

As Cicero, the Roman statesman said, *"The sinews of war are... endless money"*. This tends to be overlooked by many who talk about increasing food production. If farmers do not have access to enough money to be able to produce the food the world needs, they simply will not. Developing agriculture requires serious investments, either from individuals or from governments. Asian and Arab countries know this and this is why they have spent massive amounts of money in African and Asian countries, and in Brazil and Argentina. If farmers cannot buy the basics to produce efficiently, they will have poor harvests. If farmers cannot be profitable, they will stop farming. In order to motivate the next generation to be in agriculture, it is important to realize that being a farmer must be attractive financially, too. To get good results, there must be the right amount of money at the right time at the right place for the right purpose. The money must be aimed at producing for the market. Financing agriculture is about meeting food demand, not about producing blindly. The situation of Kenyan corn producers is an illustration of agricultural production without market access. In 2011, they asked their government for financial help, as they had difficulties selling their production. Demand for corn was strong and world prices were quite high. In such market conditions, they should never have had financial trouble. Just like there is a need for efficient market-driven precision agriculture, the future of agriculture financing must evolve to efficient food-market-driven precision financing.

Chances of success will increase significantly when development is carried out according to these guidelines. Agricultural development has had mixed reviews in the past. It is true that results have been sometimes disappointing.

There is no point in investing money if production is not developed from the market end. The market does not need to be the world. It can be the local community as well. It is a choice and it depends on how much money is available for development. If there is no market access, the farmers' profitability will be poor and their future will be uncertain. Just as collaborative leadership must function between the links of a value chain, agricultural development must take place as part of a comprehensive economic development strategy. By developing the whole economy instead of limiting action to farmers, more people will have jobs and will earn more money. For many of them, it will mean the first step out of poverty. With more people being able to afford food, food demand will increase, and farmers will have stronger markets. If their condition improves, they will stay in farming, they will be able to buy better tools and inputs and they will grow their farming activity and make a better living. As they make more money, they can also afford to buy more of the life essentials, pay for their children's education and get better health care. It will benefit other activities like local stores and services. The positive dynamics will feed the system and the economy will grow. In poor countries with a rural population of 70% or more, this represents a large number of people and a serious boost to local activity and local demand for products and services. All activities must be developed in a concerted manner. There is no true economic development and long-term prosperity without social, cultural and environmental development. Focusing only on agriculture is not sufficient. Small businesses must have the means to grow as well.

Vision is only the beginning. Actually, it is the easy part. The vision must be turned into reality. The next step for collaborative leadership is collaborative execution. Since nobody can do it all alone, the participants will have to join forces. This is where things become interesting. Considering how difficult the execution of strategies within one organization is, the level of difficulty will be multiplied, as several organizations must execute one vision together.

One of the challenges will be about the distribution of roles. One of the very first steps will be to define the areas of responsibilities and the deliverables. The roles will also evolve over time. The leadership will change as the collaborative project makes progress. It will be like an athletics relay. The baton will change hands. The person who initiated it does not have to be the person who will lead it until completion. It will depend on the skills available. The participants will have to fill in the roles in which they are at their best. There will be a need for leaders to formalize the vision and sell it. There will be a need for leaders to set up the action plan. There will be a need for leaders to execute the different actions. There will be the need for leaders to coordinate and make sure collaboration remains collaboration, indeed. The temptation of some of the deadly sins will rise inevitably. A bit of pride, greed, envy, wrath or sloth may occur. The human factor always plays a pivotal role in the execution of a plan. Following a long-term common goal while other day-to-day activities must also be carried out will create some conflicts. They can be schedule conflicts, they can be conflicts of interests, or they can be interpersonal conflicts. The leadership will have to ensure that the participants will transcend their personal agendas and keep focusing on the final objectives.

Although most action plans and business plans are quite well written, they tend to present the same flaws. Entrepreneurs and project leaders are always very enthusiastic and passionate about their plans. Enthusiasm and passion are excellent qualities that serve new activities well. However, they tend to skew the assessment of the things that may happen. The SWOT (Strengths, Weaknesses, Opportunities, Threats) analysis is often more a SwOt analysis. Strengths tend to be overestimated, while weaknesses tend to be underestimated. Similarly, the degree of difficulty to turn opportunities into reality often appears to be underestimated as well as the seriousness of threats.

A beautiful example to illustrate this is the situation of the farmed salmon industry in the late 1990s. In 1998, a study had been published asking executives from the sector to predict the future. The results of the survey showed that most of them expected a strong consolidation of the industry in the future. Many companies would not survive. When asked if they felt if their respective companies would survive the restructuring, most executives responded that, although many companies would disappear or be bought, it would not happen to theirs, because they were solid. The results of the survey show how human nature works. Of course, it is delusional for everyone to think not to be affected while expecting major changes to happen in the industry. After all, bad things can happen only to other people. By the end of 1999, the salmon market crashed, and prices would eventually plummet by half within a few months. The industry was actually solid. The optimism made salmon farmers increase production too much. Greed, envy and pride were doing well. Volumes exceeded consumption potential, and the law of supply and demand did the rest. Prices collapsed. Many companies suffered huge losses. The world largest producer was among the casualties, and it would have to sell its salmon farming operations. However, only a couple of months before the market crashed, its CEO was still claiming to investors "*the good salmon prices are expected to continue*". It is not easy to be objective about one's passion.

When other stakeholders benefit from a plan, the chances of success increase substantially. Too often, the impact of a plan on third parties tends to be neglected. The estimated value and estimated benefit for the other partners are useful to add to a plan. Such an exercise in empathy helps to look at the plan from the perspective of an outsider.

When done thoroughly, it will indicate what kind of resistance may arise that may hinder the success of the plan. Further, every plan should include a Plan B, and even a sketch of a Plan C. Murphy's law[10] never misses an opportunity to apply.

---

[10] Murphy's law: "What can go wrong will go wrong"

Many food security projects involve different cultures. The diversity of cultures may be an asset for humanity, but it often causes difficulties in the execution of actions. People learn their culture from the moment they are born. A culture is comparable to a program they receive from their parents. Its main function is to guarantee a harmonious functioning of the society of which they are a member. They act according to an unwritten set of rules without being even conscious of it. A culture affects the way they live, the way they die, the way they think, the way they perceive, the way they organize and the way they solve problems.

A Dutch scholar, Geert Hofstede[11], has done a marvelous work of studying and identifying the dimensions that shape cultures. He identified five dimensions: Power Distance, Uncertainty Avoidance, Individualism/Collectivism, Masculinity/Femininity and Long-Term Orientation/Short-Term Orientation.

Societies with a large power distance accept inequalities and hierarchy in which everybody has his/her rightful place. People high in the hierarchy are about inaccessible for those from lower levels. The ones holding power enjoy privileges. In such societies, the way to change the social system is usually rather violent. Revolution is usually the most common way to achieve change. Societies with a low power distance strive for equality within the members of the society. Hierarchy has more of a functional role than a societal one and even people in power are rather easily accessible. In these societies, social change happens through a gradual redistribution of power. They choose evolution instead of revolution.

Cultures that have uncertainty avoidance have a higher level of stress and anxiety. They accept demonstrations of emotions and aggression. Conflict and competition lead to unpredictability, so they are undesirable. Such societies have a strong need for laws and rules, for an absolute truth in science and in religion that nobody should challenge.

---

[11] Comparisons of dimensions between countries can be visualized at http://geert-hofstede.com/countries.html. This is a great way to see quickly whether particular cultures are a good match or not.

Societies with low uncertainty avoidance are much more relaxed and low stress. In these countries, they prefer to have as few rules as possible, as rules could cause rigidity. People do not show their emotions, nor do they show aggression. They accept differences of opinion and they are more tolerant. People are more willing to take conscious risks because they are less afraid of the unknown.

In individualistic societies, connections to groups are rather loose and the loyalty to the group is weak. They foster private opinion, self-achievement and self-interest. They have a universal approach to the world, and their values should apply to all. Anglo-Saxon countries score high on individualism. In collectivist societies, the individual comes second behind the group's interest. The group predetermines opinions and members have a strong sense of loyalty to the group, even if they disagree. In these societies, there is no secret. Information travels within the group almost instantly. They believe more in the particularity of groups than in a universal standard. Most developing countries score high on collectivism, therefore low on individualism.

In masculine societies, the dominant values are success, money and material goods. These societies are driven by performance and ambition. People tend to live to work and they like everything that is big and fast. Roles between men and women are separated, but women are allowed to fill "men's roles" if they think and behave like men. Anglo-Saxon countries show a high masculinity score. Feminine cultures focus more on the quality of life and on the care for others. They work to live, not the opposite. They show sympathy for the unfortunate (whom masculine cultures would call the "losers"). They tend to think that small and slow is beautiful. Women will fill "men's roles" just as men will do "women's jobs", too. Scandinavian countries and The Netherlands score high on femininity.

Values associated with long-term orientation are thrift and perseverance. Such cultures will not look for immediate results. They will patiently work on achieving long-term goals, regardless of others' impatience or pressure. Asian countries score high on long-term orientation. The USA, country of instant gratification, scores low on this dimension.

Multicultural interaction becomes particularly interesting when cultures that score on opposite ends of the various dimensions have to cooperate. Someone from a culture with a long-term orientation will find someone from a short-term oriented culture impatient and pushy, while the short-term oriented person will find the other indecisive or suspect him/her of stalling the process. Similarly, one of them does not care much about developing a relationship prior to action, while the other does. Someone from an individualistic culture will find a person from a collectivist society unreliable. Both persons will not perceive the interests at stake in the same manner. The interpersonal relationship will not have the same meaning, and the loyalty to the larger group will interfere with agreements made and confidentiality aspects. There are no secrets to be kept in a collectivist society. The group knows everything. Similarly, cultures that avoid uncertainty and that have a need for structure and organization will feel uncomfortable with someone who has low uncertainty avoidance behavior. That person will appear reckless or risky. In the opposite direction, the high uncertainty avoidance individual will be perceived as a very agitated control freak possibly bordering sometimes to hysteria. Someone from a feminine culture will see a person from a masculine society as focused primarily on money, things and status and not so much on the quality of life, care for others and for the environment. A masculine culture will find someone from a feminine culture as not driven and not competitive and who focuses on the wrong aspects of life. By combining differences in different dimensions of cultures, the number of misunderstandings can quickly add up to complete mistrust and frustrations[12].

---

[12] See the table listing some of the major countries in Appendix 3

One of the difficult areas in intercultural projects is the issue of corruption. The concept of bribe varies substantially between cultures. When is a gift not a gift? It also takes two parties for corruption to exist: the one who takes the bribe, and the one who gives it. When is giving something to a decider an attempt to influence his/her decision in favor of the giver? When is asking for gifts a prerequisite to allow the giver to get what he/she wants to get? The causes of corruption are diverse. Dire economic condition is one of them. For many people, corruption is a way of making ends meet. Others are corrupt just out of greed and power, because they can get away with it. A question that comes up regularly is how to handle corrupt people. There are three ways of dealing with the issue. The most appropriate strategy depends on the personality of the bribe taker. The first approach is to refuse corruption. It may be a matter of principle, or a matter of cultural background. The result is that the project may end there. The second approach is to make the corrupted one understand that it is a bad strategy for him/her. This approach requires influence from the one who opposes corruption. In most cases, only a stronger power position and an ability to inflict pain on the corrupt one will succeed to avoid the pitfall of corruption. It can be risky, though. A change in the relation of power can make future progress impossible. Of course, the stick is not the only option. The carrot may work better. For the carrot to work, it is necessary to identify which of the seven deadly sins are the preference of the bribe taker, and to outsmart him/her. Another soft approach is to make him/her realize how much they would miss by not working with the party who wants to develop the project. If the marginal cost of not doing business is higher than the marginal benefit of the bribe, the bribe may matter less. The third approach is to accept it. In most cases, there will be no way to oppose corruption. Competing projects or businesses may be ready to accept to pay the bribe for the sake of getting the contract. This is the situation where corruption survives thanks to the corruptor. This may be the only way for progress to succeed. The future may bring better times, but in the present only brutal realism and acceptance of the situation will make the project possible.

Understanding the influence of the cultural dimensions helps understand many of the international negotiations, be it about climate change, economic development, international trade or financial policies. These differences also explain how different countries think about the future and which actions they will likely take. Depending on whether their culture is one of open discussion and consensus or one of highly central dictatorial power, the type of action, and especially of interaction, between government, businesses and people will differ. The level of individualism and the sense of time, or even emergency, will also influence the type of decisions they will make, as well as the level of commitment.

PART IV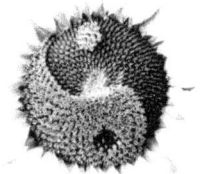

The Likely and the Desirable

Food Shapes the World

Food has always played a role in the history of humanity. It has been and it still is a weapon for some rulers to control or submit people. Food, or more accurately hunger, has been used in warfare. Starving a surrounded population has allowed many conquerors to force the decision. Hunger also has worked against the rulers. Hunger fuelled the French Revolution. The wealthy French aristocrats were disconnected from the concerns of the average citizen. They did not understand why the people revolted. It cost many of them their heads. History tells that King Louis XVI asked why his people were revolting, and the answer he got was *"they want bread"*.

Food shapes politics and policies. The European Common Agricultural Policy (CAP) is a consequence of the food shortages that the population faced during World War II. The purpose of the CAP is to ensure food security in the European Union. It has been a major contributor to the development of the EU. China emerged from a chronic situation of near famine only a few decades ago. The Chinese government clearly made the choice to feed its people. Although looking for partnerships with Western capitalists was not an obvious combination with the communistic dogma, pragmatism and the desire to stay in power by preventing social unrest prevailed. Although China has areas for optimization, higher efficiency and post-harvest loss reduction, the country is reaching its limits for production. This is partly the result of serious environmental problems, and it is partly because they already produce a lot. It is important to remember that China is the world's largest producer of rice, wheat, cotton, pork, fruit, vegetables and seafood, and it is the second largest producer of corn.

Because of the domestic physical limitations, China is eager to buy land abroad to secure its food supply. This policy has an effect on Africa where China spends large amounts of money to purchase land, but also to build a local economy by supporting the development of many small businesses and manufacturing plants. Saudi Arabia had a policy of food self-sufficiency. Until 2009, their purpose was to produce all they needed. Limited water resources have shown the limitation of this policy. To avoid the risk of having a shortage of drinking water, the Saudis have decided to buy land abroad to grow their food. This strategy is affecting the countries where they buy farmland, too. Their region is vulnerable economically and socially. In 2011, riots flared throughout the Arab world. Food prices contributed to the unrest. The process is still unfolding. The consequences may be more profound and much beyond the Arab world than it may seem at first.

As most of the wealth and most of the consumption was located in industrialized countries, the largest agriculture and food companies originated and grew strongly in these countries. The economy and consumption grows now mostly in emerging countries. Therefore, it is only logical to expect the emergence of new players in the agribusiness. The current giants will also have to deal with new competitors from the emerging countries. The strongest area of consumption is the animal protein sector. Within this sector, aquaculture has been the fastest growing activity over the past couple of decades. Human consumption of basic staples like wheat or rice is not growing as fast. The sector of grain and oilseeds will grow in the existing producing countries. Moreover, these productions are bound to the soil and climate. They cannot be relocated much. If agricultural development is done well, vegetal production will increase strongly in Africa, and to lesser extent in South America and Asia. As far as animal production is concerned, the situation is different. They can be located about anywhere and large production volumes can be developed rather quickly, especially for production with a short cycle, such as chicken, pork, tilapia or pangasius[13].

---

[13] Tilapia and pangasius are two species of fish widely produced in aquaculture. They grow fast and are relatively cheap to produce.

Animal production, and fish and meat processing, can grow quickly in new regions. In the meat sector, where the strongest consumption increase is taking place, new giants are emerging. Brazilian companies like JBS, Brasil Foods and Marfrig are already established as major players in the world of meat. Other new giants are on the rise, such as Cherkizovo from Russia or Zhongpin from China. In the future, large meat and fish companies will lead also in South East Asia and Africa. Especially in Africa, production and infrastructure are still underdeveloped, and strong growth numbers will appear in the coming decades. There will be competition from Chinese firms in the seed sector, too. China is restructuring the sector. Westerners should not think that China will accept having its food security in the hands of foreign seed suppliers. The Chinese government will make sure that they control the seed supply. The giants that will emerge will capitalize on the growing ties between China and Africa, and there will likely become a dominant force on the African continent. Arab countries will also be increasingly present and active in trade and as shareholders of food companies, such as Hassad Foods from Qatar. It is quite possible that industrial or financial groups from emerging countries will gradually buy Western companies, or that corporate headquarters will relocate closer to the future consumption centers. The new giants are likely to outperform a number of Western companies. Agribusiness corporations from emerging countries have been buying a number of European and American companies. This trend will probably continue. Asian agribusiness groups such as Olam, Wilmar, Sumitomo, Cofco and Noble are growing strongly. Some of the Western food and agriculture beacons of today will disappear. The changing dynamics and the new geography of agribusiness corporations will also influence and alter world's politics and international relations.

Consumers Shape Food Production Systems

Although it is tempting to think that food producers are the ones deciding what food production systems are, they depend in fact on the choices and the attitude of consumers. Agribusiness and farmers follow the lead of the consumers' wishes and only develop systems that produce items in demand at the lowest cost possible.

Production systems are shaped by demand. The type of production that is the most affordable to the largest number of people becomes the dominant one. Here, it is important to make the difference between cheap and affordable. Although cheap is usually affordable, affordable does not mean cheap. When food is affordable, people buy what they need and consume it. When food is cheap, consumers over-consume and throw food away what rots or passes the best before date, without the slightest feeling of guilt. Prices affect the consumption pattern. In the store, many consumers look at the price labels, and choose the cheaper alternative. Except for a minority, budgets are tight and money needs to be spent carefully. Demand for organic foods increases, but the main limiting factor is the price. If the price were the same as the "regular" foods, organic farming would very probably take over the world within a few years. Organic farming is still a niche, and its market share seems to plateau at 3% to 5% of the total food market. However, margins on organic foods are high.

As long as this same approach will remain, organic food will have difficulties passing the 5% market share mark. If organic producers and retailers were to lower their margins on organic foods to make them competitive with the regular items, the market share of organic foods would soar.

The demand is there. In the USA, Community Supported Agriculture (CSA) is growing strongly. Although aquaculture producers claim that aquaculture is more efficient than land-based farm animals such as chickens or pigs, their pricing give a different incentive. The prices of aquaculture products in the stores are higher than most meat cuts. Fish is not going to take over burgers, chicken filets or pork with such a pricing strategy.

Food is loaded with a high emotional content. It is not just about nutrition. In some cases, consumer choices are rather irrational. A few examples illustrate this. When BSE, or mad cow disease, hit the UK in 1996, beef consumption dropped sharply. However, the behavior of consumers was odd. A leading retailer put British beef on sale at 50% off the normal price. They had their best weekend sales ever by then. When asked why they had bought beef, while there were serious concerns about health risks, some consumers gave answers such as "*At that price it is worth taking the risk*" or, even better, "*I will freeze it and eat it once the mad cow crisis is over*"! At the same time, customers' visits to the leading fast food chain dropped sharply. Beef burgers were not in demand, even though their beef was from the Netherlands, a country free of BSE by then. In Europe, mostly in France, consumers used to demand white veal. Slightly pink was not good enough. It had to be plain white. To achieve this, calves were held in narrow crates and they were fed exclusively a milk powder diet. This diet did not contain iron. It kept the calves anemic, and therefore the meat could be white. After many years of this system, animal welfare activists denounced what they considered bad treatment of animals. For farmers and for the industry, the crate system was the most economically efficient system. There was an apparent conflict between animal welfare and economy. The demand of white meat with a normal diet could not be reconciled. The real problem was that consumers wanted something that does not exist in nature. It took years before consumers finally understood that veal was supposed to be pink. Once they understood that pink was the acceptable color, the market changed and calves were no longer held in crates.

It took years before consumers finally understood that veal was supposed to be pink. Once they understood that pink was the acceptable color, the market changed and calves were no longer held in crates.

For most customers, white eggs are perceived as being from intensive cage production, while brown eggs are perceived as being more "natural". Everyone with knowledge of the industry knows that the color of the shell has nothing to do with the nutritional quality of the egg. It has nothing to do with any particular production system, either. It is possible to have free-range white eggs as well as brown eggs from intensive cage husbandry systems. The shell color is just like hair color or eye color in humans. It depends on a gene. The belief that the egg color indicates a difference persists, though, and prices are different.

Some blind tests carried out between "industrial" and free-range chicken meat carried out in the Netherlands in the 1980s produced interesting results. When consumers were not told which was which, they could not clearly taste a difference, while when they knew which meat was from which production system, they overwhelmingly gave the preference to the free-range chicken.

Who, with a rational mind, would choose to eat junk? Yet, junk food is quite popular in North America, and it has been a growing trend in many European and emerging countries as well.

The list could continue and certainly, everyone has more examples of irrational consumer behavior. Consumer demand, both the rational kind as the irrational one, determines what farmers and food companies produce and sell. In this regard, consumers share a great responsibility in what is produced, how it is produced, where it is produced and how it is distributed to them. Blaming retail or agribusiness alone for the kind of food systems that are in place is easy and unfair to some extent, although the industry advertises to create new consumer needs to deliver a return on new product development. Markets work in a particular way. If people buy something repeatedly, someone will keep producing it. If consumption stops, so does production.

It would be interesting to imagine what people would eat if they were rational, and what the impact on food production systems would be. A rational diet would follow proper nutritional recommendations, and to this extent would follow the same principles as those used in animal nutrition. However, this would not have to be as boring a diet as what farm animals are fed. A rational diet does not need to be a ration. The art of cooking prepares delicious rational meals. It would be like having the best of both worlds. The emotional, social and hedonistic functions of food would remain. The key would be about balance and moderation. If people were eating rationally, there would not be any diet-related illnesses. There would not be obesity. There also would be much less food waste. This would improve the level of sustainability of agriculture.

Will consumers become more rational in the future? Probably not, but they will become better informed and more critical over time. Especially with the rise of social media, information circulates much faster and trends can gather momentum faster than in the past. More programs for healthier eating are currently running and action is taking place at many levels. In particular, schools are a place where much can be achieved. One can wonder how long the lunch money and self-service system will last. Having schools placing vending machines selling items that are highly unbalanced foods and leaving the decision to children to decide what they want to eat was of course a disaster waiting to happen. Nobody can realistically expect children to consistently make the choice of spending their lunch money on broccoli and mineral water. Kids will choose what they like best, not what is best for their health. They need adults for guidance. The duty of adults is to teach children what is right and what is wrong. Unfortunately, too many parents fail at that.

Attitude towards food is changing all over the world. Currently, two major trends are growing. One is taking place in North America and the other is happening in emerging countries.

In North America, consumers are starting to question the way their food is produced. This is a major change compared with their attitude until a few years ago.

Until the early 2000s, American consumers simply seemed to consume without trying to know much about production methods. Hormones, antibiotics or GMOs seemed to be accepted. A more accurate statement would be that North American consumers did not care. This was a sharp contrast with Europe, where all of the above had already met strong resistance from consumers, retailers and governments for a couple of decades. Then, the BSE crisis scared them all. The dynamics of the change of attitude of North American consumers is very reminiscent of what happened in Europe during the 1990s. Consumers are losing trust in government agencies, and retailers seem to be the ones to champion food quality, traceability and production methods. The fight about GMOs is in full swing and it is getting only more vivid, in the USA and everywhere else. This will have much more profound consequences in the way food is produced than agribusiness seems to realize, or is willing to admit. The population is aging, the generations are changing and the values about food are shifting. The current opposition is not a short-term fad. Consumers will make different choices. Some food producers see that and are already adapting, but many producers still seem to think that opposition will pass. They are in for a surprise. The expressed plan of Wal-Mart to buy more from small and mid-size farms, to reduce waste, to ensure food safety, to make healthy food affordable and to develop sustainable sources of agricultural products is a very clear signal that the food business environment is changing. The retailers and large food service companies have the size and the power to influence change.

In emerging countries, consumers are changing their eating habits, too, but for a different reason. They now have more disposable income. The previous subsistence diet made of mostly grain, such as rice, wheat or corn, are now including more animal protein, as well as fruits and vegetables. In these countries, consumers are not overly critical of their food production and distribution systems yet, but issues that arose in developed countries affect the way food is produced, especially in the area of food safety.

These consumers probably would like to experience the same level of food security and affordability of food as has been the case in the West over the past five decades. Whether this trend will continue is uncertain. The higher demand for animal protein and for biofuels tends to create food inflation. Food prices will be firm at best and they are more likely to increase in the future on an ongoing basis.

There is no doubt that consumers and retailers are increasingly going to put the emphasis on sustainability, health, food safety and transparency. This may sometimes lead to conflicting objectives with the need to produce more food globally. This does not need to be a problem, but this is why the world needs strong leaders to show the way towards meeting both objectives of better food and of more food.

While many debates continue in the political and parapolitical world about many aspects of food production systems and the impact of human activity on the environment, retailers and restaurants lead a quiet revolution. Without making the headlines, they gradually change the way their suppliers will do business in the years to come.

Such an evolution is certainly welcome, especially in a time where important decisions need to be made. Political leaders seem unable to reach any effective agreement on environmental issues, as the world could see at the late climate summits of Copenhagen and Durban. In the food sector, there are many discussions going on about sustainability and genetic engineering, to name the two hottest items, but the political class does not seem to generate clear and concrete action plans.

Just like what happened in the 1990s in food safety in Europe, retailers are taking the initiative to create momentum in the current issues. The problems that plagued the food industry in Europe, such as salmonella in poultry, mad cow disease, or dioxin in Belgian fat for chicken feed showed a number of weaknesses that needed to be addressed.

In the case of BSE, British retailers did not wait for British or European legislation to demand meat and bone meal-free feed for farm animals. These were dramatic times.

Tough decisions that had serious financial consequences had to be made on very short notice. By then, a couple of reasons made the retailers took the lead. First, the inability of the UK government to prevent and tackle the issues was creating a bit of a vacuum in leadership. Consumer confidence in their institutions was fading, and retailers were the only ones, true or not, perceived to take the proper actions to protect the public. The second reason was the fact that many retailers had their own private labels. In this case, the problem was not the supplier's problem anymore, because the supermarket chain could have risked serious damage to its reputation if a food safety issue had been associated with its brand.

Today, retailers are again in the position where they can present themselves as the consumers' champions. Legislation is slow to move and to make significant decisions. The involvement of interest groups adds to the fight and complicates decision-making. To prepare for the future, they already have come out with plans and communication on how and where they want the food they sell to be produced, and they try to offer a choice to consumers. By doing so, the most active among them are setting new standards, and forcing the whole production and supply chain to think about the things to come.

In the recent past, new initiatives indicate that retailers are pursuing further on such initiatives. Wal-Mart came with their plans as indicated previously. In the UK, Sainsbury committed GBP40 million to invest in farming. In France, Carrefour, the world's second largest retailer, launched the "Reared without GMO" program. In their stores, they sell 300 food items labeled as being GMO-free, to offer consumer a choice based on transparent information. If Carrefour ventures into this, one can be sure that they do so because they already know that this will be good for their business.

If they gain market share, it is very likely that their competitors will soon react by issuing similar programs. The EU Commission may be struggling to figure out how to deal with GMOs, but Carrefour says "Let the consumers tell us!" Vox populi, vox dei![14]

Retailers are not waiting anymore for politicians to make decisions. They have defined their vision, they know what they want and do not want, and they are passing the message on to the suppliers. What would happen in agribusiness USA if American retailers and restaurants took a similar approach as Carrefour? The ties between retailers and social and environmental non-profit organizations are getting closer and closer. The trend is clear. Retailers and foodservice will decide eventually on all issues related to food safety, agricultural practices, environment and social impacts, not the agribusiness. Because of the pressure from the consumers, retailers and foodservice, all other controversial products and production techniques will eventually be eliminated and replaced. Agribusiness will only produce at the lowest cost possible for the new standards. Cheap is on the way out.

In the years before the current economic crisis, the non-profit sector was already creating more jobs than the for-profit sector. In 2010, the total of all operating budgets of non-profit organizations passed the US$1 trillion mark. This amazing number seems to have been unnoticed, yet it has quite some significance for the way the economy might evolve in the future. They are a force to be reckoned with. They tend to have a higher moral status image with urban consumers, especially compared with the for-profit sector. Nobody has the monopoly on morals, but non-profits have a PR advantage in this area. A part of their strength comes from the loss of trust in government, science, industry and politics by the public. In the food and agriculture sector, the influence of non-profit organizations is growing, and it challenges the way food is produced.

---

[14] Latin for "The voice of the people is God's voice"

Just as in the for-profit sector, the size of non-profits as well as the quality of their message varies. Just as it is the case with some corporations, the integrity of some non-profits is sometimes questionable. However, in order to motivate individuals and organizations to donate money, they need to have and to keep enough credibility. Competition exists in the non-profit sector, too. Only the ones that do the best job can survive. Nonetheless, non-profits have been instrumental for many changes in food production. It is also clear that change and improvement in production processes comes only from being questioned and challenged. Industrial processes are based on standardization and low cost. Industries are never looking forward to changing their processes especially when change comes with an upfront cost.

A first example comes from The Netherlands. The largest Dutch supermarket chain, Albert Heijn, part of Ahold, the fourth largest retailer in the world, will sell only pork produced in animal friendly conditions, according to a protocol set up by Dierenbescherming, a non-profit organization dedicated to humane animal treatment. The meat group Vion, one of the largest meat companies in Europe, will supply the meat. This situation did not happen spontaneously. In the Netherlands, 25 years ago, the situation was quite different. At the time, all Dutch pork processors were suffering large financial losses. They were desperately trying to offer a meat produced with better feed and in better husbandry systems. All the large suppliers had approached Albert Heijn to develop a market. Albert Heijn had carried out some consumers surveys. The results were encouraging. About 80% of the consumers answered positively to the question of whether they would be willing to pay more money to have better meat. Unfortunately, when shopping in the stores, the consumers acted very differently. Because they did not perceive any difference at the meat counter, the price remained the main variable, and all the projects of better pork through this sales channel failed. In that same period, an activist organization was constantly challenging the intensive meat industry. They were considered extreme and unrealistic about the realities of meat production and meat consumption by the industry. The industry did not even want to engage in a discussion with them.

The name of that organization was… Dierenbescherming. Since then, all the large pork producers that were trying to develop the better pork have been through a number of mergers and acquisitions. They eventually merged in one large group. The name of the group is… Vion. How things can change in 25 years! The main difference is that 25 years ago, the industry's approach was marketing-driven, and nowadays, the change is market-driven. The difference between the two approaches is that the former is a push strategy, while the latter is a pull strategy. What happened in the Netherlands is not an isolated case.

Still in the pig sector, the HSUS (Humane Society of the United States) is fighting fiercely against what they consider inhumane treatment of pigs, especially gestation stalls for sows. The HSUS is a non-profit organization strongly opposed to intensive animal husbandry. They want to end factory farms. The HSUS and the US meat industry are not friends. They have opposite views on animal husbandry and meat production. They accuse each other of the usual shortcomings and lies, as is the case between industry and its opponents. All the rhetoric and the arguments are the same as those used in the Dutch case a couple of decades earlier. The dynamics are the same and it is no surprise to see that the HSUS is booking victories. They have a strong influence and their approach resonates with retailers and foodservice.

Because of their actions, American fast-food companies and retailers have decided to ban supplies from farms that would use the tight gestation stalls. The pig industry expressed its satisfaction for what it considers the result of its leading role in this change, which to their satisfaction was not because of government.

In the egg sector, the HSUS has come to an agreement in 2011 with the United Egg Producers to work together for federal law to keep hens in cages up to twice the current size.

Greenpeace is one of the most active organizations that try to change how food is produced. To say the least, the food and agriculture lobbies are not too enthusiastic about their actions, but Greenpeace gets things changed.

They addressed the issue of beef production in Brazil and its relation to deforestation. They achieved more than the Brazilian government by reaching agreements with beef producers in a region where the "law of the gun" tends to prevail. It has been the result of the influence of Greenpeace on the main fast food companies and retailers. They have pledged not to buy beef that would be produced at the expense of deforestation. The pressure of the customers of the beef producers, who also want to show their environmental concerns to the consumers, weighed heavily in the decision. The prospect of losing a major part of their business has quite some leverage on the Brazilian producers' mindset.

A similar situation occurred in the production of palm oil in Indonesia and Malaysia. Greenpeace's action to save the orangutans' natural habitat has resulted in large users such as Nestlé and Unilever purchasing only sustainable palm oil products. This has more impact than government action. Another non-profit with influence on food production is WWF. Together with Unilever, they created the Marine Stewardship Council in 1997, which goal is to set sustainability standards and conduct certification of fisheries. In 2009, the WWF created, together with the Dutch Sustainable Trade Initiative, the Aquaculture Stewardship Council, which has a similar mandate as the MSC, but for aquaculture. The Dutch Sustainable Trade Initiative states on its website *"There are two kinds of companies: those that sell sustainable products and those that will"*

These are just a few examples, but they show without any doubt that the message of non-profit organizations has a strong and growing audience. With environmental issues becoming common media material, their influence will only increase.

It is also clear that, increasingly, retailers, foodservice and, to a lesser extent, consumer goods manufacturers are joining them. The businesses with direct contact the public are leading this change. Of course, where there is change, there is resistance. The reaction of the food industry is normal in this process. The winners of tomorrow will be the companies that understand where the business environment is heading, and that will see the opportunities to implement change faster and better than their competitors will.

We Will Reap What We Sow

Markets Will Reach a New Equilibrium

Demand for agricultural products is increasing strongly in two areas: animal protein and biofuels. It happens at a pace that is challenging the ability of the farmers to keep up with that demand. The result of this new balance between supply and demand is higher prices. The higher demand for animal protein and for biofuels will drive the dynamics of the entire agricultural sector. These products require more raw materials, which are mostly grains and oilseeds. Future food prices will depend on the ability of agriculture to feed farm animals and cars.

Several scenarios are possible. The first one is the most favorable one: the farmers find ways of keeping up with the higher demand by producing adequate volumes and the balance between supply and demand does not change significantly. Prices remain rather stable. Everything is fine. Unfortunately, this scenario does not seem to be the most likely one, in the short term at least.

Then there is the second, much more exciting, scenario: the farmers cannot keep up with demand. As demand for animal products and biofuels increases, human nature will manifest. The first reaction of the meat, fish, dairy, eggs and biofuel producers will be to try to meet the demand. They will increase their production capacity. They will do that without really confirming that the farmers who produce corn, soybeans, and other animal feed ingredients can keep up. The increase of production capacity will strongly increase demand for agricultural commodities. Since it is unlikely that commodities producers will have developed a detailed plan about how high the demand will be in the short term, demand will outpace supply.

The price of agricultural commodities will increase. The price increase will be the trigger for commodities farmers to plant more. When prices are stable or declining, they have less incentive to produce more.

The first to feel the pain will be the producers of animal protein and of biofuels. The price increase of agricultural commodities will translate to the increase of the price of animal feed for animal production and of feedstock for ethanol production. Animal feed represents 70% of the cost of production of animal protein. The price increase of grains may have an unexpected effect for beef production. If the supply of corn cannot meet the demand, the relative part of corn used for beef production will decrease. It is likely that corn will reach a price at which grass becomes more competitive and attractive. It would not be a surprise if grass-fed beef becomes more competitive than corn-fed beef. Ruminants are the only way to transform grass into food for human consumption. Since the world's area of grassland is twice as large as the area of arable land, using grass to feed cattle and to replace some of the tight grain supply would be a good move from a resource management point of view. All producers of animal products will have to cope with substantially higher costs. As usual, passing the price increase to consumers will take time, as retailers will resist. Retailers want to keep attracting consumers to their stores, not deter them from buying. No retailer will want to be the first one to increase prices and risk losing business to a competitor. They will try to keep meat prices stable for as long as they can. Of course, if the price of agricultural commodities is to stay high, consumers will inevitably have to accept price increases for food in general, and for meat, fish and other animal products in particular. Depending on the processors' ability to generate acceptable margins, the sectors of animal production and biofuels may undergo some restructuring and merging activities to improve their financial results. There will be plant closures.

As food becomes more expensive, consumers will look for the more affordable alternative first. At first, they will try to keep the portions at the same size by switching between alternatives. The cheaper meat will suffer less than the more expensive one. This will probably benefit chicken consumption compared with pork or beef. Also within a particular species, consumers may switch the parts of the animal they buy, such as replacing steak with ground beef. They will go for cheaper cuts. They also will buy smarter and hunt for bargains. Impulsive purchases will be less frequent, unless the product is very cheap. If keeping the size of the portions at par does not work, then they will buy slightly smaller portions or buy less often. People will slightly reduce their food intake of the ingredients that cost the most. Those who were over-consuming might actually benefit from a positive impact on their health. For those who already were struggling, this will be more difficult to deal with. Of all the food sorts, animal protein will be the most affected by an increase of the price of food commodities. Already in 2011, there are clear signs from meat and poultry companies that the price of feed is seriously squeezing their margins. When a business is not profitable, there is a correction happening. If producing animals is losing money, producers will reduce their volumes. This is exactly what is already happening. US production of beef and chicken will decrease in 2012. US meat consumption already did. The same is expected to happen in the EU.

As production decreases, and by still not planning ahead in a market-oriented manner, a temporary and relative surplus of grains and oilseeds may occur, which will ease the prices of agricultural commodities. Crop farmers will make less money than for instance in the excellent 2011 season. They will be less tempted to increase their production further. Then, it all will depend on how animal protein producers act. It also will depend on how much financial pain they suffer. They will not boost their production unless their profitability improves again. If the price of agricultural commodities drops, animal protein producers will not pass the cost decrease to the consumers. They will keep it to improve their financial results.

Consumers will not be enticed to buy more as the price of animal products will remain at the previously increased levels. There will be a status quo of the value chain in terms of volumes as long as the animal protein producers do not return to a profitability that will entice them to increase production. When profitability returns, they will increase their volumes again. For some time, prices will be stable. When margins become good enough again, they will push production volumes further. By then, depending on whether crop farmers, animal feed companies, and animal protein producers have taken a market-oriented approach for future planning, the same situation will happen again. Demand for agricultural commodities will increase again, stimulating crop farmers to plant more. The cycle will continue. However, as the world will have more consumers, fluctuations in supply and demand will have more effect. The result will be an ongoing increased volatility of agricultural markets and of food prices.

Animal production and ethanol are activities that can be planned rather accurately. They take place in controlled environments. Production of grains and oilseeds takes place in the outdoors. They are much more subject to external factors that are difficult to predict and to manage, such as climatic conditions or pests. Nonetheless, they can influence largely the availability and the price of raw materials. There will be years when prices ease, and there will be years with food inflation. Considering how much work will be required to increase vegetal production, it is likely that there will be more years from the latter category for food prices, though. The financial performance of animal protein producers will also suffer more vicissitudes than the performance of crop farmers. The producers of vegetal agricultural commodities should be rather profitable for years to come. Of course, there will be lesser years, but it is reasonable to expect their financial position to be comfortable.

Food markets will not be affected only by the level of the demand for animal products and for biofuels. The price of inputs will affect the financial results of farmers and food companies.

A whole system based on cheap commodities is about to change, simply because there will not be any cheap commodity anymore. Energy, fertilizers, crop protection products will all become more expensive. These are all adjustments to rebalance consumption behavior from the unbridled overconsumption of the past decades, when consumers from rich countries were not thinking much about the consequences of their actions. The industry will figure out how to increase efficiency to contain some of the cost increases.

The prices of meat, dairy, eggs and fish are going to be affected by other factors than just feed prices. The need for more control on food safety issues, a lower use of antibiotics, lower densities of animals on farms and stricter environmental regulations will increase production costs for animal husbandry, aquaculture and fisheries. The change of farming practices will make meat significantly more expensive than it is today. The days of ad-lib cheap meat are ending.

The future dynamics of food prices as presented here will be ongoing. As long as diets do not adjust to a new equilibrium, meat will keep increasing faster than other basic food staples, until meat consumption, and therefore meat production, will reset to different levels. It will not happen overnight. It will be a gradual process. There will not be any meat or fish riots. If food riots happen, they will be about the basic food staples, simply because the first ones to riot will be the less affluent consumers, whose diet consists mostly from rice, wheat, corn, cassava or potatoes, depending on where they live.

When Externalities Become Visible

Externalities are costs, or benefits, that are not included in the price charged for a product. If a cost is not included in the price, it represents a negative externality. If a benefit is not included, the externality is positive. The concept of externality is particularly important to determine whether an activity is sustainable. For instance, if an industrial activity pollutes and causes harm, there will be consequences, and costs. As it takes many years for environmental problems to become obvious, the cost of repairing the damage caused by pollution is not included in the cost of the goods produced by the industrial activity in question. However, there will be a day when it there will be no alternative but to clean the damage. That cost is the externality. Every activity that pollutes without cleaning the contaminants is a negative externality. Everything that damages physically the environment and undermines the sustainability of food production is a negative externality. Every activity that depletes essential resources for the production of food is a negative externality. In this highly industrialized world, the consequences of economic and human activities slowly add up. Nature's resilience makes it possible for damage to remain unnoticed for quite some time. However, the ability of Nature to repair the damage shrinks, as the damage is continuous and exceeds Nature's ability to cope with the problem. As the population increases, the level of human and economic activities intensifies further. There will come a time when Nature simply cannot handle the damage and repair it in a timely manner anymore. The buffer will be full. When this happens, the effect of negative externalities will manifest immediately, and it will include the cumulated damage over decades as well. It will feel like not paying the bills for a long time and then having all belongings repossessed. Humanity will feel stripped and highly vulnerable.

The advisory services company KPMG published a report in 2012 stating that if companies had to pay for the environmental cost of their production, it would cost them an average 41% of their corporate earnings. These costs are currently not included in the pricing. That is how high negative externalities can be. Looking at it from the other way, companies would still deliver 59% of their current earnings. Repairing the damage and still generating profits shows that sustainability is financially achievable. On average, the profits would only be lower, but the impact would vary substantially between companies. Businesses that create high negative externalities will show much bigger drops in profit than business that do the right thing. The only ones who would have to get over some disappointment would be Wall Street investors and all those who chase capital gains on company shares. The world could live with that. Investors should put their money only in companies that actually have a future.

All the fossil fuels that humans burn are gone forever. They are not renewable. All the water that farmers use for food production and exported away from the production region is gone forever. Exporters in arid regions will have no choice than to disappear, produce only for the local markets or, if it is economically sensible, import water from surplus regions. All the minerals that are used as fertilizers and that are exported from the fields in the form of leaching or in the form of agricultural commodities are gone forever. New supplies produced with either non-renewable energy sources or from mines that are slowly depleting must replace the loss.

Organic matter that is lost from soils must be replaced, or it will be gone forever. Soil that is lost through erosion and climate is gone forever, unless new soil is brought back on the land or very long-lasting repair techniques are applied. Every gene that is lost is lost forever and might be missed dearly. Every species that goes extinct is gone forever, as well as its role in the ecosystem. Every molecule of greenhouse gas that goes into the atmosphere is gone out of human control forever.

Since everything that becomes rarer also becomes more expensive, the externalities are going to weigh on the economics of food and agriculture, as well as in any other activity. There will be an oil price for which the current machines will be too expensive to operate, and for perishables to be too costly to truck with fossil fuels over long distances. The economics of water will change the purpose of farming in arid regions. It will alter the agricultural policies and force farmers to innovate new irrigation techniques. The economics of minerals and organic matter will change the location of animal farms and manure containment systems. No minerals will be lost. Manure will become a competitive fertilizer, as chemical fertilizers will become much more expensive to produce. The logistics of manure will change and the location of animal farms will change to allow an optimal cost efficiency of raw material for feed and access to fertilizing elements and organic matter. Farms will not have to be mixed, but the agricultural landscape will restore an integration of crop farms with animal farms. Agriculture will be sustainable only if it completes all the cycles. In the past decades, the cycles of minerals, of organic matter and of water have been open. Food has been produced in one place, and then moved over long distances and the waste and surpluses have accumulated somewhere else, while the original production areas were slowly depleting. New systems and new organization will work on closing the cycles again to bring back what agriculture needs to function.

The economics of energy will change the chemical industry and its products. Everything will aim at using as little primary resources as possible and maximize the efficiency of inputs by both bringing entirely new products and application techniques. It will be true for energy, water, fertilizers, chemicals and medicines.

The new focus will be on using just what is needed, when it is needed, only in the dose that is needed, and no more than that. It will be all about precision agriculture, precision animal husbandry, precision packing, precision manufacturing, precision processing and precision logistics.

When externalities manifest immediately, there will no time discrepancy between financial results and environmental results. There will be no excuse anymore to say that there is no evidence of consequences. There will be no possibility of creating confusion, either. When pushed to the limits of its resilience, Nature will bring the financial and the environmental at the same timeline. It will be stressful. Doing the right thing environmentally, or in other words, producing sustainably, will be the best and only short-term strategy for financial sustainability.

If a linear approach to the economy is not sustainable, another model needs to emerge. If the consumption society is approaching its end, what will be the next society? Circular thinking brings part of the answer. As recycling and reusing will become part of manufacturing processes, it should become an integral part of consumer behaviors, too. The future will be about looking at consumption goods in a different manner. The end of the consumption society would not mean the end of consumption. What would disappear is the attitude of buying more stuff than really necessary, and that eventually end up in the landfill. The shift from always more to always enough will have to create an economy of loops that have to be closed all the time to ensure the reusing and recycling of goods.

A new time has come. The priority must now be quality before quantity. People must think about having enough, not having always more. This thinking is not nostalgia to a past that also had its limitations. It is not about rejecting a market-based economy. It is about looking at the market that has always been here, but that has been pushed in the background for the more convenient approach of only producing and selling more.

What will be brought to market are not so much products as services. These services are the ones that are directly related to making all the natural and industrial cycles run harmoniously in a durable way. All activities around cleaning the damage that humans have caused, and all recycling activities will become more and more important in the economy.

In the same way, water treatment is going to be a crucial activity, even more so than it has been so far. Clean industries producing durable goods and services will prevail.

Such a change will make some jobs disappear. It will make other jobs appear, or even reappear. As usual, change always brings opportunities. It is necessary to recognize them and to take them. The time has come to make the transition from this consumption society, based on wasting resources, and with no future, to a maintenance society where prosperity, not growth, will be the economic success indicator. By acting today, this process can happen in a smoother way than by waiting until there is no choice anymore.

There is so much to maintain and to repair. A few decades ago, before society started to throw away almost everything, repair and maintenance activities were an integral part of the economy. The difference was that consumption goods were not cheap. Some were more affordable than others, but they were not cheap. People appreciated their value and wanted them to last as long as possible. In the mass consumption society, lasting has been actually a disadvantage. What does not last has to be replaced more often. Buying replacement means sales, which in turn means higher GDP. Unfortunately, the GDP has become the main indicator of the health of the economy. This approach is questionable. To make a comparison with a business activity, GDP would be comparable to the sales revenue of a company. To assess the value and the health of a company, sales revenue is a poor indicator. It may give an idea of how dynamic the company is, but other important parameters are missing. A better indicator of the health of a company is the profit. Profit is the surplus of money that sales have created after paying all the bills for products and services that helped produce and sell the company's products and services. However, there is more than profit. A good cash-flow position is essential for any business. If the cash flow is always negative, the company will end up in bankruptcy.

For a country, the equivalent of profit and cash flow would be the sum of all the businesses profits and cash flows, and all the households' savings. Profit would be the increase of money on all bank accounts of the country's population and economic actors. This would be a better indicator than GDP to assess the wealth of a nation.

In business, there is another very interesting indicator, called the economic value added, or EVA. The EVA is the profit minus the cost of financing the company's working capital[15]. The cost of financing the capital is what it would cost a company if it took a loan to finance its working capital. Introducing a concept similar to EVA to assess a country's economic performance would be interesting, even more so in the current times of money printing, skyrocketing debt and budget deficits.

Another important indicator for the health of a company and the commitment of its workforce is the employee turnover. It is not included in the profit and loss account, although it certainly contributes to its results. Employee turnover is a good indicator of employee satisfaction, and of the good management of the company. A well-run business where people love to work has low employee turnover. People are happy to work there and want to stay there. They are more productive. They are less sick. They hardly complain. Happiness pays off. Moreover, they stay in the company because they believe in its future. This should be every politician's dream. For a country, the equivalent of employee turnover is the emigration rate. Most people leave their country when they have no hope left and they see a better future abroad than at home. It would be interesting to map the world with such a happiness index and compare it with the usual GDP indicator.

---

[15] Working Capital is equal to Account Receivables plus Inventory minus Account Payables. The higher the working capital, the higher the need to finance the company's operations. A well-managed company aims at having the lowest working capital possible, by getting paid as quickly as possible by customers, by lowering the level of its inventory, and by paying suppliers as late as possible (through favorable payment terms).

If the economy shifts from a purely volume-driven GDP approach to a more maintenance-driven quality of life index, one can wonder what is there to repair and maintain since the habit is to replace things. The answer is simple. There are plenty of things to repair and maintain. A quick look at infrastructure in many countries gives an idea of how much work is needed.

To give a few simple and clear examples, the state of roads, bridges, railways, electric grid is quite poor in some parts of the world, and that is true in developed countries, too. In developing countries, infrastructure needs to be built. Of course, the challenge is to finance such projects from the national budgets. However, money considerations aside, the need for maintenance is there. It would create many jobs. It would stimulate the economy. The leaders need to find the funding. A good infrastructure is critical for the proper functioning of a society. The need for recycling is also huge. Landfills are full. In the course of 2011, the UK indicated that it had run out of landfill space.

The dramatic pictures of children in developing countries who sort out trash from garbage mountains show that the waste has some value to some people. The conditions are sordid and show what desperation and poverty cause. Nonetheless, there will be an increasing need to take out what has been stored. Today's landfills will be the mines of tomorrow. There is a future for economic activity and for job creation. Now is the time to think of creating more jobs. In all the discussions about the landmark of nine billion people on Earth, there are many questions about how to feed them, but about none about what work will they have. Supposedly, 70% of the world's population will live in cities, but nobody is asking what all these people will do for a living in there. To buy food, they will need money. To have money, they will need decently paying jobs. An essential part of the answer about solutions to hunger depends on future economic activity. Will populations concentrate in cities because that is where the jobs of the future will be? It would be ideal and a sign of a prosperous economy. It would be a job-market-driven change. The alternative would be a further flow of people who flee from poverty and hunger that increases urban poverty.

It is worth reflecting on how the labor market will evolve in the future. Many jobs have changed locations. The manufacturing that served the large consumer markets of Western countries moved to low-wage countries.

Companies offered cheaper goods and boosted their profit margins by employing people who would accept conditions that Western workers would not. Many industrial activities have left the West and are now in Asia, South America and, to a lesser extent, Africa. In particular, such a move fuelled the economic boom of China. The result of relocation is the emergence of the middle class in emerging countries. This new middle class is becoming wealthier. The economic boom also brings some inflation. The local wages that were so low until a decade ago are now increasing. In the West, the middle class is disappearing, and the economic situation of many households is uncertain. In these countries, the population is aging and the birth rates are low. There is no baby boom going on anymore. The proportion of active people in the total population is decreasing. All benefits, entitlements and social programs are more difficult to fund. In Western countries, the problem to solve is how to create jobs that pay the good salaries that can compete with developing countries, while keeping social benefits at the same level. The answer is that the current status quo will not be possible any longer. Governments have to take more debt to fund their social benefit programs. This is not sustainable, especially when the number of taxpayers is not increasing at the same pace as the need for funding. It is very likely, that to re-create economic growth, wages will have to decrease, workers will have to accept less comfortable benefits, the retirement age will have to go up and pensions and other benefits will have to be lower. The world of labor is going to readjust itself slowly. Wages are going to converge. In developing countries, they will increase. In developed countries, they will decrease. The differential will shrink, and a number of industrial activities will probably return to the countries they left. This process will take time. If wages in China are going up, other parts of the world have even lower wages to offer. In particular, this should benefit Africa.

The African continent could be where the next economic boom will take place. Manufacturing may gradually leave China and relocate in India, Southeast Asia and Africa. In the meantime, developed countries need to reinvent their economies. Since they cannot expect to bring back the lost manufacturing soon, they have to look at what activities cannot be relocated. That is where the strength of a new era would have to be. Only jobs that are physically impossible to relocate will offer a strong future. The idea of having the low-paying jobs going away being replaced by higher-paying jobs in technology and know-how that would stay in developed countries is a fantasy. Developing countries learn new technologies fast. China and India have nuclear weapons and send satellites into space. They understand rocket science just as well as Western countries. Every year, they produce more graduates than the West does. The West is not going to keep ahead in knowledge, science and technology for very long. The intellectual and scientific dominance of the West will disappear, and will gradually shift to Asia, South America and, later, Africa. Everyone who has spent time with students from emerging countries knows how enthusiastic, knowledgeable and smart they are. Students from Western countries do not seem to have the same drive. Westerners should be more curious and show more eagerness to learn. The winners will be those who are hungry for knowledge and who are enthusiastic about creating the future. Professionals from the new economic powers will fill all these highly qualified jobs, and for lower wages. What cannot be relocated away from the West are jobs linked to the land, such as agriculture and resources. They are jobs linked to local communities such as construction, infrastructure, maintenance and tourism. They are jobs linked to local people, such as healthcare and personal services. A similar trend will also emerge in developing countries. China is the example of a place where social and environmental maintenance will be badly needed. The future economy will be about care and maintenance. Maintenance will be the new economic driver.

For any form of pollution, contamination or damage due to industrial activity, it is possible to imagine a form of maintenance activity. As mentioned before, financing such activities is the challenge.

In a society focused on consumption goods, the assumption is that disposable income can have only the purpose of buying goods. In this approach, taxes are perceived as money being diverted from the commonly accepted dominant source of GDP.

What would happen if the purpose of money changed? How would the economy change if money were not spent on consumer goods that deplete finite resources that end up accumulated in landfills or, in the case of food, end up as body fat? If people spent less, they would save more, but they also would have more disposable income to pay for maintenance activities. Of course, the term "maintenance activities" could mean taxes in the case that they would be performed by a government organization. It does not need to be the case for everything. Private companies can also perform maintenance. The jobs that disposable income would support would not be retail and manufacturing jobs anymore, but they would be maintenance jobs. Shifting the focus from consumption to maintenance requires a change of mindset, especially about the purpose of money. Maintenance is a collective benefit. Consumer goods are an individual benefit. The change of mindset is really one from self-centered to altruistic. Such a shift can be challenging, but it is not impossible. Placing the collective before the individual is not a bad thing. After all, acting collectively has helped the human species to dominate the world. A human being alone would not survive long on his own. The need for social bond is still strong. It has become virtual, as it has become online, but it is still present nonetheless. The social media boom is the best proof. People want friends, even thousands of them if possible as their Facebook page can prove. They want someone to talk to, or to text to. The need for social fabric is actually very compatible with the need for maintenance and collective benefit. It will be necessary to re-create a different connection. The brands will not have to be about shoes, clothes, sunglasses or cars. The new brand may be the nice neighborhood, region, country, or more idealistically, the planet.

What does it matter if jobs are in retail or in gardening or in construction? What does it matter if jobs are in factories, in offices, in plumbing, in health care of in agriculture? It does not matter, as long as people have a function in the society and that the society functions well. It does not matter as long as they can make a decent living. It does not matter as long as they are happy about themselves. A happy society is a society that services the most important needs of the citizens.

If the consumption society is over, and if it is not anymore about volumes, one can wonder what the future strategies of businesses should be. First, with more than two billion more people on Earth in the coming four decades, especially in countries with a growing middle class emerging from poverty, there will be growth. The end of the consumption society will not be the end of consumption. It will be the end of excesses and waste. Individual consumption will decrease, but the number of people will compensate for that. It will be a different type of attitude, which will result in a different type of products and services. In the food sector, nobody should ask of obese people to eat more food in the future than they currently do. It is physically almost impossible, and it would be sadistic. Moreover, encouraging people into a lifestyle that undermines the health of the population, or contributing to it, is not patriotic. It undermines the future resilience and dynamism of a country, not to mention that the health costs are also diverting precious money from projects that actually serve future prosperity. Consumption will not grow in the West. It will grow in the currently emerging countries. Food companies will have to adapt to different customers with different cultural backgrounds. As linear thinking disappears to be replaced by circular thinking, sales volumes will become less strong indicators of growth and of financial performance. The circular thinking will bring companies to bring more service in their products to meet growing needs and requirements for recycling and reuse.

Gradually, they will "internalize" the externalities. This will drive further profit improvement. The focus will shift from a production-driven volume approach to a profit margin market-driven one.

Forecasting from both market demand and the ability of agriculture to keep up will play a central role to develop sustainably profitable strategies. There will be a rebalancing from commoditization towards specialties. The same shift from "always more" towards "always enough" that consumers need to make will have to happen for agriculture and food companies, too. Evolution is an ongoing process.

An Uncertain World

The world is evolving rapidly. The world economy is shifting and political leadership is being challenged. Suspicion about corporations is growing. Demographic pressure and climate change add to the uncertainty.

The riots in the Arab world received a lot of coverage. This is good, because the problems in this region have been ignored for a long time. In 1987, the late French economist Alfred Sauvy, the man who created the term "Third World" published a book called "*L'Europe Submergée – Sud-Nord dans 30 ans*[16]". His book was a description of the demographic and economic differences between Europe and the nations from the South, and of the likely consequences. He predicted that within 30 to 40 years, Europe would see a flow of immigration from the other side of the Mediterranean Sea that would replace the original European population. He also saw in this migration a great opportunity in terms of economic renewal for Europe.

In most Arab countries, half the population is younger than 25. This is in sharp contrast to Western countries where almost half the population is older than 40. Then, what to think of Sub-Saharan Africa where half the population is younger than 20? When the riots erupted in Tunisia, it was really striking to see the pictures of rioters: they were teenagers. What a sharp contrast with the Greek and other European demonstrators who look like a mob coming from an elderly home!

---

[16] The title means "Submerged Europe – North-South Relations in 30 years"

With chronic unemployment, especially among the youth, and many people living on a pittance, it was not a surprise to see riots, and governments being toppled. This situation has been going on for a few decades. A new generation is coming of age. They are ready to start and to support their own families. They need to have prospects for their professional lives, but there is no work. A difference with other past social unrest is that many rioters actually come from the middle class. Many young protesters are quite well educated. These riots are not proletarian. They are the sign of an economic dead end. The message to the rulers is clear: change must come or change will come. The lesson is hard for Arab countries and they are now more aware than ever of how precarious their situation is. This is also a loud warning to the rich nations. At first, they did not hear it. At the 2011 Davos World Economic Forum, the elites were not even aware of what was going on. Eventually, they heard it and paid attention. Stock markets dropped for one day only as unrest was spreading in Egypt.

Interestingly enough, markets were up on the days that a bomb exploded in Moscow's airport, and when Standard & Poor's downgraded Japan's economic rating. Certain things matter more than others. Europe must now realize that, unless it helps its southern neighbors solve the problem, they are going to become a part of it. North Africa, just like the rest of Africa, needs economic development. The people of these countries need to regain hope in the future. Now, they are not optimistic.

Development and stability is in the interest of rich countries, just as much as it is for developing countries. Europe, Russia and the USA cannot thrive with countries on the verge of collapse at their borders. Many borders have originated from agreements between the superpowers at the end of World War II. Many other borders are the result of the dismantling of the former European colonial empires. They have not been drawn based on ethnic or geographic reasons. It is likely that many borders will change.

Many other borders are the result of the dismantling of the former European colonial empires. They have not been drawn based on ethnic or geographic reasons. It is likely that many borders will change.

Tribal, ethnic and religious local conflicts are good indicators of the changes to come. Many borders will be redrawn, new countries will appear, and some may disappear. It will take place in the Middle East, in Africa, in Arab countries and in Central Asia. A number of regions contain a demographic time bomb waiting for a food security problem to explode. One is the area between Russia and the former Central Asian Soviet republics, extended to Iran, Afghanistan and Pakistan. It probably will affect India as well. Another is the border between Mexico and the USA. Law and order are getting increasingly difficult to maintain in Mexico. The European Union has many issues to solve. Its functioning and membership will evolve. New dynamics may appear, especially around the Mediterranean. The role of Turkey will be interesting to follow. Other economic or political unions will appear. They may bring back to life the contours of former empires, such as the Ottoman sphere of influence. The bond between Russia and other Slavic nations and other traditional allies is strong. The resource-rich Kazakhstan lying between Russia and China has an interesting geographic location. These regions are going to have to work together to find strategies to ensure stability. This probably will not happen without skirmishes. The political situation will change. Many of the countries where booming demographics, poor economic situation and precarious food security are the normal state of affairs need a 21st century Marshall Plan. Regions in Western Africa and in Eastern Africa are also vulnerable and conflicts will occur and spread over borders.

The potential for feeding the world's population is there, but the main cause of hunger is the lack of affordability of food. In 2008, there were food riots, but there was no real food shortage. The main problem was that the populations could not pay for it because the price had skyrocketed, especially the price of basic food staples such as rice, wheat and corn. In 2011, food prices were even higher than in 2008.

Yet, there has not been the same kind of riots. A reason for this difference may have been the fact that retail prices of food staples remained somehow contained. The price increase affected mostly animal feed, animal production and biofuels.

Unfortunately, the answer to the question of whether there will be food riots again is yes. Although there is much political talk about food prices and risks of riots, nothing is really done to prevent it from happening again. It does not look like there is much political will to make the necessary reforms to prevent extreme tensions. To many people, most world forums and summits of all sorts look more like an opportunity for the wealthy and powerful to hobnob than a place where actual decisions are made. Regardless of whether this is true or not, frustrations are growing. The WTO Doha Round, which if completed well could deliver many solutions, takes forever to come to a conclusion. It is highly likely that the world, and mostly the rich nations, will understand the message and act only when they will feel that their position is in danger, too. Food riots will come as soon as food affordability drops under an acceptable threshold of pain. Of course, Asia, Latin America, Arab countries and Africa are the most likely candidates for such unrest, but rich countries are not immune to that, either. In particular, the USA is more vulnerable that many may think. In 2008, when food prices skyrocketed, and although there were no food shortages in the USA, it only took a rumor to trigger a rush to stores, hoarding and even a few fights between shoppers. In 2009, the USDA estimate of households that do not have enough money to feed themselves was 14.6%. In 2011, there were about 46 million American on food stamps. Although the economy seems to have stabilized, it has not recovered yet. Moreover, the housing situation in the USA is far from stabilized. Many Americans have been able to keep consuming because they simply stopped paying their mortgages and could stay in their homes. The number of mortgage delinquencies is so high that banks cannot handle all the cases. Actually, most cases have been postponed, but one day, some decisions will have to be made.

If the banks played by the book and foreclosed on all houses of owners who cannot pay their mortgages, there would be an incredibly high number of homeless broke people. The banks would have to report serious losses. How would these people manage to eat then? The risk of inflation is serious, as financial markets play the commodities only to hedge against the loss of value of the dollar. Inflation in an economy that is fragile will reduce the affordability of food for the less wealthy.

If demographics and economy have the potential to reshape the political map, so does climate change! If the sea level is to rise as indicated by many experts, the coastlines will be altered, and the amount of land above sea level will shrink. The populations of the submerged areas will have to relocate. The pressure will be the highest in countries where the density of population is high and where food security is low. This will bring economic, human and political problems. The flow of climate refugees and migrations will not be domestic problems. They will affect the international community. It will affect food supply, as many delta areas produce large amounts of food, rice in particular. The root cause of climate change already triggers a flow of migration of an unusual kind. The heavy air and water pollution is the reason why a number of affluent Chinese are emigrating to cleaner places. They buy properties in the USA, Canada, Singapore and Europe. The Bank of China and the Hurun Report published in late 2011 the results of a survey of 980 Chinese millionaires. The results show that 46% are considering emigrating or have already emigrated.

In this world full of imbalances, in the distribution of population, in food security, in economic situations, in wealth distribution, in pollution, in soil degradation, in future opportunities, corrective action needs to take place or Nature will take care of it. Nature sets the hardware. Humans can do nothing to change it. However, they can develop the software. The software is everything that encompasses human ability. The components of the software are economy, science, technology, morals, philosophy, spirituality, laws, trade, industry, services, rules, culture, analysis, leadership and action.

Globalization makes the exercise both easier and more complicated. It is probably because globalization has been mostly an economic phenomenon. It has been mostly about production and consumption of goods and services. It has not been about human synergies. Humans are social animals and they need to know where they belong. In the past, the local character of the economy and of most human activities made things simple. Mobility was rare. People were attached to their villages, to their countries, to their social groups, to their cultures, and to their jobs. With the emergence of globalization, job relocation and mobility, the world feels more uncertain. The feeling of belonging for life to a larger group has been shaken. There used to be a time when companies had a nationality. They were American, British, Japanese, French, Italian, German, etc... With the rise of multinationals, only the headquarters are linked to a country, but the different operating companies are spread over many countries and are being relocated when it suits the corporation. The nature of the loyalty of companies to employees and the loyalty of the employees has changed. The old concept of a job for life at Forever-With-Us Ltd has gone. People will have to change careers several times in their lives. In the past, companies had a local character. They were the main economic drivers in a region, and they used to be family-run. The family was usually from that particular region, too. Large companies do not operate like this anymore. The physical bond with the territory of origin has disappeared. The relationship between government and business, especially big business, has evolved. There is one major difference between the two, though. If multinational companies are diffuse and spread around the world, governments are linked physically to a territory and to a population. Countries cannot fire their citizens. They have to deal with social issues. Countries cannot relocate. They must deal with environmental issues. Countries cannot close. They must focus on long-term objectives. Governments and businesses have different functions. The verb to govern comes from the Latin gubernare, which means to steer, to direct and to rule. The role of a government is to create the proper set of rules to create the conditions for a prosperous society to develop.

A government defines the laws. It determines what is acceptable and what is not acceptable in its society. It creates the conditions that ensure an orderly society. A government is the guardian of civilization. A government works for the collective good. A government does not run a business, but it sets the rules for business to operate according to the values of its society.

Businesses have a different function. Businesses are not there to govern. They are there to offer the goods and services that contribute to the prosperity of societies. They operate according to the rules set by the governments. The role of a business is to be economically viable, and it must be managed accordingly.

In the ideal world in which governments and businesses focus on their respective areas of responsibilities, societies should be more prosperous, more orderly, socially stable and environmentally sustainable. When businesses start to interfere with politics, the collectivity starts to suffer. Political power shifts to unelected influencers. Elected officials cannot govern properly. The prosperity of the society becomes second to the prosperity of those who have influence. When governments interfere with business management, businesses do not perform as they should and the economy suffers. Prosperity is not at its optimum. The people start to manifest their dissatisfaction.

This is when the civil society starts to play a more visible role. The civil society is embodied by environmental and social non-profit organizations. It acts to pinpoint the shortcomings and the lack of collective and long-term focus of governments and of businesses. It reminds them what their duties are towards society. In a sense, the civil society plays the role of a conscience reminding the influencers and deciders of the consequences of their decisions, or of the lack of it.

Regardless of whether the messages and arguments of the civil society are right or wrong, science-based or not or rational or not, they carry the voice of those whom they represent. In a democratic setting, the voice of the civil society is just as good as anyone else's. The truth is always in the eye of the beholder.

Because the roles and the relationship between governments and businesses have shifted from their original, and ideal, ones, the odds for problems to occur are higher than they would be otherwise. Crises have an amazing ability to shake complacency. Crises will make governments intervene more strongly for food security, and do what they are supposed to do. The only unknown is the cost of procrastination.

Governments, businesses and civil society are essential for a society. Those who think that there should be less government must remember that anarchy literally means no government. Without businesses, there would be substantially fewer jobs and fewer goods to meet the needs of the population. Without a civil society, the only option for the silent majority to have its voice heard would be revolution. All three stakeholders are necessary, and even more so when future food security is at stake. Perhaps the most difficult challenge for these stakeholders is to operate in a multinational world. Businesses and non-profits have moved from the local to the global a few decades ago. National governments have not and they cannot. If the world wants to find a harmonious balance, the concept of nation and the essence of government may need to change. It can be only successful if people can relate to a group. The risk of exclusion or of isolation of individuals in large numbers will trigger resistance. Businesses will not take care of citizens. It is not their mandate, at least not today. However, somebody needs to take care of the basic functions of government and of its duties to citizens.

Rethinking the World

The scope of influence has shifted. Individual countries have more and more difficulties acting effectively with issues that have become global, or at least international. The economy has globalized, companies look at their business from their multinational point of view. Environmental and social non-profits have the same international approach. For many issues, the interests are not local anymore. The new situation also requires a new approach of sovereignty and of problem solving.

The world is gradually rebalancing in many areas. The differences in salaries will level off in the end. Wealth will be better distributed geographically because of the emerging middle class in Asia, Latin America and Africa. There will be less poverty. The issues of climate change, international trade, food security and water security are global. They cannot be solved effectively by having individual nations acting separately. Global issues need to be solved globally as well as locally. Climate change discussion will not succeed as long as it focuses on individual national greenhouse gases emissions. The blame game is counterproductive. It must be solved collectively. Setting targets on individual nations will not work. One of the main arguments used by countries is always that they will not act unless others act, too. Chinese emissions of CO_2 because of its use of coal affect everyone, and China is in this situation because of Western consumer markets. Who is to blame, then? It is not possible to point a finger. Companies in China are not all Chinese. Many are multinationals. The reality is that everybody is responsible for the problem, but nobody is big enough to fix it. Issues like climate change need collaborative leadership to be solved. National interests are almost irrelevant. A global plan is necessary.

International trade discussions are also quite laborious to say the least. It is difficult to set fair rules in a world where discrepancies in terms of labor force, capital and resources are so big. As the discrepancies shrink, many of the difficult discussion topics will fade away. Water security also raises international issues. When some water systems cross several countries, the consequences of decisions also flow to the neighbors. If countries divert water away from their neighbors, it is only natural to expect them to complain. If a country pollutes water, the neighbors will complain, too. Water management is going to become a matter of collaborative solutions. It will become international. Food security also requires a collaborative approach. It is necessary to produce food optimally everywhere it is possible. It is important to solve as many local problems as possible, because the issue has global repercussions. What happens in one part of the world affects prices and affordability in other parts of the world. Failure to develop certain regions undermines the production of adequate supplies for the whole world. It affects populations and it has the potential to create serious conflicts. The issue is international.

With such different stakeholders having scopes of influence, and therefore of interest, that are so different, a new distribution of areas of responsibilities is necessary. Since most problems seem to revolve around borders, a fresh approach would be to imagine a world without borders. What if there was only one world of soon nine billion people? There would not be countries anymore, therefore there would not be multinationals, either. The entire world would be just one big entity. The idea may be difficult to fathom at first, but thinking about what the advantages might be is a stimulating exercise. If the planet were only one country, population densities would readjust more harmoniously.

Overpopulation creates areas of pollution and scarcities of clean air, clean water, productive soil and food. These problems persist and worsen because borders make migrations difficult. Immigration issues exist mostly because of borders and national interests. One world would offer the advantage to the aging nations of benefiting of the youth from other areas to contribute to their retirement and health plans.

Theoretically, there could be many advantages of unifying the peoples of the Earth. However, history has shown that the concept of nations is resilient.

Until now, most of the attempts to unify the world have been acts of war, but they all had the same objective. They have been attempts to bring together large amounts of resources under one leadership, based on one vision. Conquests have also been the way to make a particular country stronger. A look at the map of the world through the centuries shows that borders are not carved in stone. There have been many changes, and it is only normal to expect more changes to happen. Many regions have evolved from feudal structures to much larger entities. Over time, many structures have been created to achieve supranational goals. The United Nations, the G8, the G20, the WTO, the European Union, the African Union, the League of Arab States, ASEAN and Mercosur are well-known examples. The EU is an attempt to bring its members under one economic entity to be stronger, but its problems show that bringing together different economic situations under separate sovereign entities can cause serious trouble. Other countries have been founded on a federative basis. The USA, Canada and Germany are such examples. There is a need to create groups with tighter ties, but very often, they have been built only around languages or cultures. The next step still has to come. Canada is a country where people from all cultures, nationalities and religions of the world coexist peacefully around a set of rules that promote tolerance, respect and equal rights. Perhaps it will be the model for a future world federation.

If the world were one, all the rivalries, disputes and conflicts between countries would disappear. There would be only one set of rules for trade. There could not be any import tariffs and there would be only one policy for subsidies. Instead of having every country trying to produce as much as possible of everything they need, the one-world agriculture would focus on producing enough of everything where it makes the most sense, economically, environmentally and socially.

It would be very interesting to compare the land use between the two situations. Instead of having 193 countries setting 193 agricultural policies, only one would be needed, and would be set to benefit all. It would require coordination and optimization based on the huge variety of climates, soils, water access, landscapes and populations. Having one big policy would aid in setting priorities better between the regions where further development is needed. One united Earth would mean one policy for the allocation of financial resources.

Carrying out the exercise of envisioning one united Earth would have the advantage to spot the hurdles that are created by the existence of borders. By removing the negative effects of international relations and of wealth disparities between countries, the actual practical problems would become more apparent. The static would go away.

As a united world is not going to happen in the foreseeable future, the exercise would also help to see how to improve the current situation. It would help create a set of recommendation by region and define a list of priorities to develop the productions that the world will need in the coming decades. It would support discussions to improve the trade of agricultural goods. Food security in the future will require a market-driven open trade, instead of a production-driven protectionism, as it is the case too often today. Similarly, the issues of subsidies would show that it is more important to harmonize them and keep the productive ones than trying to remove them all at all costs.

Although it is highly unlikely that the Earth unites any time soon, it is essential to realize that future success will depend on solidarity and cooperation. It is a radically different approach than the consumption society and its desire for individualistic instant gratification.

The most frequent questions about the future of food and farming are "*How can we feed the world?*" and "*What will farming look like in the future?*" These questions reflect the linear thinking that dominates today's thinking. Undoubtedly, identifying trends and connecting the dots of all the data and information available brings some interesting answers. One question seems to be missing, and yet it is an important one: what do we want food and farming to look like in the future? It is disappointing that this question comes up so rarely. Answering it is really a good basis to develop a vision, to stimulate innovation and to have constructive discussions. Reflecting on what we want farming and food to look like in the future has many advantages.

Answering the question is about developing an ideal vision of how it should be. It is about eliminating all the unsustainable practices. It would be about breaking up with the baggage from the past and re-creating agriculture. The point of such a brainstorming exercise is about presenting wishes before being about feasibility. In a first phase, there is no point in putting a price on everything. That will come later. The exercise produces a draft that will be open for comments, remarks, reactions, objections and additions. Once this part is done, the principle of action and reaction will apply in full mode. Then a dialogue can take place. It is important to put the discussion in the perspective of some timelines. Envisioning the future of food and farming is not something that has to happen at once. If the vision relates to several decades ahead, one must remember that many things will change. On the one hand, it may allow things that are impossible or unpractical today to become reality in the future. On the other hand, change will make some practices become unsustainable and they will disappear.

The dialogue can then focus on how to make the vision work, instead of trying to decide now if it can work. The discussion can develop around what is needed and how much time it might take to make the vision reality. It would explore the necessary changes that should take place in the human environment, such as rules, policies, leadership, technology, financial resources, human resources, attitude of the society and of the people.

To envision the future and to adapt to it quickly, the mind needs stimulation. Humans have demonstrated through the centuries how resilient, creative and resourceful they can be. Usually, these qualities shine in periods of crises. When life is comfortable enough, people tend to become complacent. Comfort always feels as if it will last forever. Doubting is already a sign of discomfort. The most successful endeavor or most successful people are not necessarily the ones that have of the most resources at their disposal, but they are always those that are the most resourceful. With this understanding that resourcefulness increases when resources become scarcer or more expensive, it is possible to develop interesting alternative scenarios to look for innovative solutions. What would happen if the world did not have enough oil, enough water for irrigation, enough fertilizers, enough crop protection products, enough land or enough money? What solutions could exist to do more with less, and can it be done? One of the first answers that come to mind is to be more efficient, and to avoid waste. Solutions will be about reducing, reusing and recycling as much as possible. Everything will become something useful for something else. People would not throw anything away anymore. This is exactly what people used to do. They were thrifty because everything was scarce and expensive. Food was not wasted. The waste was used to feed animals... to produce food. Even in periods of plenty, the reflexes of difficult times are the most appropriate to keep abundance continue. In parallel to brainstorming on future possibilities, it is necessary to review the current situation. Since nothing is perfect, it is good to identify the current practices it would be desirable to eliminate in the future, and think of new ones to replace them.

The purpose of this book is not to carry out such a brainstorming session and to present an almost endless list of questions. When people have total freedom to think of solutions, the number of ideas that arise is amazing. People know and can do much more than they usually think. Brainstorming is much more effective and more enjoyable when it is done "live" within a group. The exercise must include all the stakeholders of the whole value chain, and of all the other economic sectors that interact with food production.

In an ideal world, what should be the attitude and the eating habits of consumers? How would it be different from today? Why do they consume more calories and protein than they actually need, and how can they change their behavior? The answers to all these questions indicate what changes in consumer behavior will mean for food companies and farmers. The changes that would take place on farms would affect their primary and secondary suppliers. It does not stop at suppliers. The questions will then involve governments at the local, national and global levels. Shaping the ideal future will inevitably question the effectiveness and the relevance of many regulations, or the lack of it. Some regulations and policies would have to be amended or terminated, and some others would have to be created. Since it is only an exercise, the discussions and negotiations of the participants do not have the same feeling of urgency and they are not as threatening as in real life. In this stage, the interaction is only a game. There is no pressure of short-term financial interests. There is no passing or failing. There is no winner or loser. Removing the greed factor and the fear factor from the discussion is the great advantage of brainstorming to create the future of food and farming. Depending on the creativity of the group, great ideas will arise. The following phase is about testing the feasibility of the new situation and about identifying all the issues, practical and financial, that are still ahead.

CONCLUSION

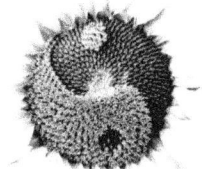

What Is Next?

What Is Next?

Today's world and tomorrow's food security is in a paradox situation. In the past, famines were always the result of food shortages. Today, famines occur in a world of plenty. The world gets fatter. In more and more countries, people eat more calories and more protein that they need. Yet, one billion people are hungry. Affluent consumers, retailers and restaurants in rich countries throw away obscene volumes of food. Yet, one billion people are hungry. In developing countries, farmers produce food, but it rots and it is lost between the farm and the consumer, because of deficient infrastructure or because of lack of proper access to market. Yet, one billion people are hungry, and mostly in these very countries. If nobody fixes these aberrations, the world could end up in serious conflicts, not because of food shortages, but because too many people eat and waste too much, and because infrastructure remains underdeveloped. There is no advantage in the status quo. It is bad for health, it is bad for the environment and it is bad for the wallet.

Many people treat their cars better than they treat their bodies. They would not use the wrong fuel or use anything that could harm the engine. They would not try to put more in the tank than it can contain. They would not forget to replace oil and risk blowing a gasket. They would not forget to change tires when they are worn out. Their cars are too precious to them for that. Apparently, their bodies are not. Nobody would throw banknotes in the garbage voluntarily. Yet, throwing food away comes down to exactly that. Nobody would ignore a banknote on the sidewalk if there were one. Yet, post-harvest losses come down to exactly that. The amount of money that can be made by fixing the problem is amazing.

It is time to educate consumers about nutrition, and to start at school. It is time to re-educate the parents to feed their children properly. It is time to understand the difference between nutritious foods and treats.

Treats are not for snacking on day in day out. Treats are supposed to reward good behavior. Eating well is neither difficult nor expensive. Apparently, it only requires a bit of discipline. Occasional excesses do not cause harm, but excesses all the time are bad. It is so bad that it may cause the current generation of children to have a lower life expectancy than their parents' do, as expected in the USA. That is not exactly the gift of life. There is nothing wrong with having a healthy lifestyle. There is nothing wrong with moderation. One may not like it and choose a different path. Those who do so must take responsibility and accept the consequences of their choices.

Responsibility is the key word. We are all responsible for what happens, either because we make it happen or because we let it happen. However, responsibility seems to have become a dirty word. It is a pity because being responsible is the sign of means growing up. It seems a difficult concept in societies where people want to look and stay young forever. Consumers want to consume without thinking of what will happen next, and when it does, they try to get compensation for what anyone with an atom of common sense knows was bad in the first place. Disclaimers rule. They are a great way to shift responsibility to someone else. The product is potentially dangerous but since that information is on the label, the supplier is not liable. This is too easy and too convenient. When the harm is done to Nature, this is a different game. Nature will not sue. Nature will not complain. Nature will simply change the environment we live in. If we do not fit in it, that will be too bad… for us.

As natural resources are being depleted, the atmosphere is being altered, the soil is being lost, the water is being contaminated, the human species is now at a crossroads. It is impossible to deny it. The time is not for pointing fingers and blaming anymore. What a waste of time, energy and money that is.

The time has come to reflect on what we want for our world. It is time to reflect on what we want for the coming generations. It is a time for dialogue, and everyone must participate. Those who do not take part in this will have to accept the course set by those who did.

The debate is not about throwing away the progress of the past. It is about adapting to a new situation and about seeing how we can enjoy the progress made, but without all the threatening consequences. Politicians of all sides, businesses and all other organizations with a social function have contributed to past adaptation. There is no reason why this generation should fail, unless it has lost completely any sense for its future. It is about looking for better alternatives. There is a myriad of opportunities to grab. There are fortunes to make by making today the strategic choices for a better tomorrow. Resistance to change is futile and will make it only more difficult and painful in the future.

To have a future, it is necessary to prepare for one. There is no point in sticking to the past. It will not help. The dinosaurs will end up in the graveyard. We must learn from the past, though. The lessons learned before are there to help us not repeat the same mistakes. That is the basis for a better future.

Today is the time to make choices. The choice is simple. It is between prosperity and chaos. It is between life and death. This is like an ancient Greek play. Mother Nature sets the stage. We, humans, cannot change it, but we write the script. We have enough knowledge to figure out what is good for us and what is not. We will decide if the play has a good ending or if it is a tragedy. Every day, we sow the seeds of tomorrow, and we will reap what we sow.

Dialogue, communication and knowledge transfer is what this world needs. They are the pillars for a better future. It is amazing to see how many organizations try to reinvent the wheel or to duplicate research work done elsewhere before. Very few people seem to know where to find information developed by others that is already available.

In these uncertain times, it is essential to have fresh opinions. When people have spent many years within a certain organization or in a certain school of thinking, they tend to become blind about their own area of expertise. All issues, especially the difficult ones, must be addressed. Denying them or postponing action will not make them disappear. It is only making them worse. It is possible to live in sustainable societies.

Farming depends too much on the effect of other industries on the quality of the air, on the climate, on the quality and availability of water and on soil preservation and improvement, on the ability to maintain a proper biodiversity and avoid the emergence of resistant monsters to act alone. Agriculture can be sustainable only if all other activities are. Just like agricultural development and hunger relief both depend on economic development at large, agriculture can only exist as part of a sustainable world.

Our knowledge will help improve technologies. However, it is necessary to realize that technology and machines are only as useful as the ones operating them. Technology is a solution only if we use it well. Technology does not mean not thinking anymore or acting mechanically. Machines are only tools to serve us. We must be careful not to reverse the roles. Considering how addicted people are to their cell phones and computers, machines may have already the upper hand. At all times, we must use our intelligence to avoid the pitfalls of convenience and complacency, as true costs come later. Nothing is free. The bill simply does not come immediately. For the future of food and farming, there is no shortage of technological solutions. Technology is part of the solution, but the key ingredient is and will remain the human factor. Whether the world will feed itself for generations to come or not depends on humans making the right choices and doing the right thing.

Shaping the future requires a good dose of foresight and a clear vision. Leaders need to have the ability to anticipate. Reacting is not a good approach. Reacting means acting after the facts. Anticipating means acting before they hit us. A simple comparison is boxing.

A boxer who knows how to anticipate will dodge on time, and will not receive harmful blows. A boxer who does not anticipate well will react. He will throw punches, but only after he has been hit and hurt. He is not as precise. His punches do not have the same impact. He may win, but his performance will be very tiring and energy consuming. Regardless of the result of the match, he may have suffered long-term injuries and he will need more time to recover than the one who floats like a butterfly[17].

Sports have rules for players to follow, and sometimes to break. Everything in society has rules, too. The system is not carved in stone. We create it and we can change it. It is our decision. If we make doing the wrong thing more attractive, people will do the wrong thing. If we make doing the right thing the better alternative, things will improve.

What does it take to make the right thing the better choice? Some short-term sacrifices will probably be necessary. That will be the tough part. This is why leaders need to have a strong vision and to be able to sell it. Thus, people will understand and accept the sacrifices. It will take courage, and courage is one of the qualities of great leaders.

We must remember that we get the leaders that we deserve. We need to be demanding, because the future will be only as bright as our leaders.

To succeed in feeding the future world's population sustainably, the first thing is to believe in the future. Negative messages only undermine action. There is only one way to make others believe in the future. We must repeat relentlessly that it is possible. We must become enthusiastic about succeeding. We also must make very clear what the price for success is.

---

[17] From the famous quote by former heavyweight boxing champion Muhammad Ali

To succeed, we must change our behavior. We must change the way we consume. We must change the way we do business. We must change the way we look at ourselves, at others and at the environment. It is a small price to pay for prosperity. We can choose not to change. Either way, we will reap what we sow!

APPENDICES

Appendix 1: Number and percentage of undernourished persons

Years	Number of people malnourished	Percentage of the world's population
2006-2008	850 million	13%
2000-2002	836 million	14%
1995-1997	792 million	14%
1990-1992	848 million	16%
1979-1981	853 million	21%
1969-1971	878 million	26%

(Source: FAO)

Appendix 2: Yields of corn and soybeans over 1970-2010

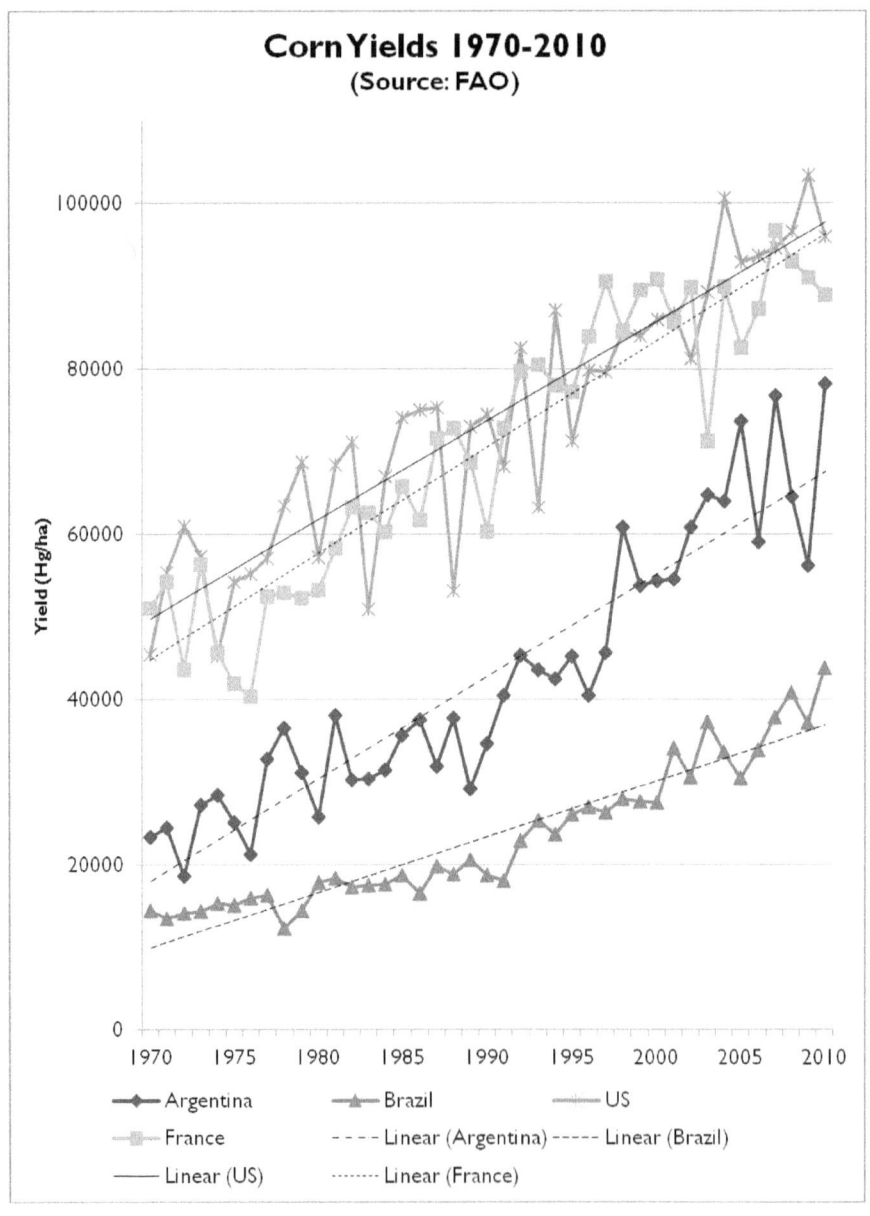

Appendix 3: Countries' scores in the five dimensional cultural model of Geert Hofstede

	Power Distance	Uncertainty Avoidance	Individualism	Masculinity	Long-Term Orientation
Brazil	high	high	low	medium	high
Argentina	medium	very high	medium	medium	very high
Chile	high	very high	low	low	N/A
Uruguay	high	very high	low	low	N/A
Mexico	very high	very high	low	high	N/A
Iran	high	high	medium	medium	N/A
Turkey	high	very high	low	medium	N/A
India	high	medium	medium	medium	high
Pakistan	medium	very high	very low	medium	N/A
China	very high	medium	low	medium	very high
Japan	medium	very high	medium	very high	high
Thailand	high	high	low	medium	medium
Indonesia	high	medium	very low	medium	N/A
Philippines	very high	medium	low	high	low
Vietnam	high	low	very low	medium	very high
USA	medium	medium	very high	high	low
Canada	low	medium	very high	medium	low
Australia	low	medium	very high	high	low
New Zealand	low	medium	high	medium	low
UK	low	low	very high	high	low
France	high	very high	high	medium	N/A
Spain	medium	very high	medium	medium	N/A
Netherlands	low	medium	very high	very low	medium
Germany	low	high	high	high	low
Denmark	very low	low	high	very low	N/A
Arab World	very high	high	low	medium	N/A
East Africa	high	medium	low	medium	low
West Africa	high	medium	low	medium	low
South Africa	medium	medium	high	high	N/A
Russia	very high	very high	low	low	N/A

We Will Reap What We Sow

About The Author

Christophe Pelletier is one of the world's experts on the future of food and farming. Born the son of a butcher and the grandson of a vintner, he was destined to food and agriculture. He obtained his Master of Science degree from the Institut National Agronomique Paris-Grignon in France, now renamed AgroParisTech, where he specialized in Economy and Development in Animal Production. During his studies and versatile professional experience, he has been active in beef, dairy, animal feed and nutrition, pork, poultry and aquaculture. His functions have ranged from scientific and technical support to extension services, sales & marketing, and senior executive management. By taking a market-driven approach, hiring talents, building lean teams and by setting clear strategic objectives to his staff, he has turned around money-losing operations into best-in-class successes within months. Christophe has conducted business on four continents with farmers, traders, wholesalers, leading agribusiness companies, leading retailers and leading food processors. He speaks English, French, Dutch, German and Spanish.

Christophe created *The Food Futurist* in 2009, first as a blog dedicated to the future of food production and food supply. The approach of the Food Futurist is to look at trends with a critical mind and without prejudice, nor bias. Christophe is available to speak at industry, government, non-profit organizations and university conferences. He organizes and leads thought-provoking seminars about shaping the future by stimulating critical thinking about innovation and interactions between food production and demography, economy and environment.

Christophe also offers strategic foresight for customers to envision and shape their future and business consulting on market-driven food value chains and business organization.

When not speaking or writing about food and farming, Christophe can be found cycling up mountain roads or running around in his kitchen, where he cooks gourmet meals for less than five dollars per person, and he bakes delicious bread.

He currently lives in Vancouver, British Columbia, Canada.

More information is available at www.hfgfoodfuturist.com

www.ingramcontent.com/pod-product-compliance
Lightning Source LLC
Chambersburg PA
CBHW051448170526
45166CB00001B/163